POCKET PORTRAITS

J.R.R. TOLKIEN

The Father of Modern Fantasy

DON MARSHALL
@DONMARSHALL72

ADAMS MEDIA
NEW YORK AMSTERDAM/ANTWERP LONDON TORONTO
SYDNEY/MELBOURNE NEW DELHI

TO MY WIFE.

Adams Media
An Imprint of Simon & Schuster, LLC
100 Technology Center Drive
Stoughton, MA 02072

First Adams Media hardcover edition
November 2025

ADAMS MEDIA and colophon are registered trademarks of Simon & Schuster, LLC.

Interior design by Kellie Emery
Illustrations by Kim Arrington
Interior images © Adobe Stock/ warmworld, Helga

Manufactured in China

10 9 8 7 6 5 4 3 2 1

Library of Congress Control Number: 2025940320

ISBN 978-1-5072-2417-5
ISBN 978-1-5072-2418-2 (ebook)

Table of Contents

Introduction

Widely regarded as the Father of Modern Fantasy thanks to his creation of the literary world of Middle-earth, J.R.R. Tolkien gave readers a place so rich with detail and adventure that they still return to it again and again seven decades later. His books, like *The Hobbit* and The Lord of the Rings trilogy, are beloved across the globe, and have been adapted into blockbuster films so popular, they're rewatched by fans every year. But you may be surprised to learn that there is more to Tolkien than hobbits and wizards . . .

In *Pocket Portraits: J.R.R. Tolkien*, you'll dig deeper into the history of this renowned author, whose own life was just as fantastical as the tales he created. Here, you'll explore one hundred biographical vignettes that peer into the world of J.R.R. Tolkien, from his early years in South Africa, to his lasting impact on pop culture. Uncover details about:

- His kidnapping as a newborn baby
- The marriage to his first (and only) love, Edith, and the efforts by the priest who tried to keep them apart
- The writing of his first major success, *The Hobbit*, during his years as a professor
- His creation of *at least* fifteen constructed languages, including two different versions of Elvish
- And more

You'll also find excerpts from several of his works, including books like The Lord of the Rings trilogy and *The Silmarillion*, stories like "Leaf by Niggle," and poems like "Bilbo's Last Song" and "The Adventures of Tom Bombadil."

From his years as an orphan, to his experiences with two World Wars, to his friendships (and competitions) with fellow authors like C.S. Lewis, Tolkien had no shortage of inspiration for his literary adventures. He crafted vivid characters and places that captivate readers to this day. An author, a philologist, a professor, and a poet, he left an enduring mark on literature, and the depth and craft of his daring tales have captivated readers over and over again. Turn the page to unravel the life and talents of the Father of Modern Fantasy.

Mabel and Arthur

John Ronald Reuel Tolkien's father, born in 1857, was named Arthur Reuel Tolkien. While many of his relatives followed in the family business of selling pianos, Arthur decided instead to pursue a career as a bank clerk. The industry wouldn't keep him in England for very long. Upon taking a job with the Bank of Africa in 1889, Arthur found himself moving to a wildly different part of the world: a place called Bloemfontein in the Orange Free State, which is now a part of South Africa.

THE MORE YOU KNOW

The name Tolkien is thought to derive from the German word *Toll-kühn*, meaning "foolishly brave" or "stupidly clever." However, some scholars disagree on exactly where the name comes from.

At the time of his move to the opposite end of the world, Arthur (then thirty-two years old) was engaged to Tolkien's mother, nineteen-year-old Mabel Suffield. A resident of Birmingham, England, Mabel was the second of seven children to John and Emily Suffield. Two years after her future husband immigrated to Bloemfontein, Mabel spent several weeks at sea on a ship called the *Roslin Castle* to join him over 8,000 miles away from Birmingham. Shortly afterward, in April 1891, the pair got married in South Africa. Their home, Bank House, was several hundred miles from Cape Town and had been provided by the Bank of Africa.

While Bloemfontein was a stark contrast to England, it had a hospital, a library, two churches, a small park, markets, and a tennis club—all comforts that made it a spot for the Tolkien family to live sufficiently. But it was also surrounded by grasslands: a hunting ground for wolves, jackals, wild dogs, and occasionally even lions! The weather was also an adjustment, reaching extremes of intense heat and bitter cold.

Despite the rugged terrain and harsh weather of South Africa, Arthur, whose health had often troubled him in England, seemed to thrive there. By all accounts, he was a happy man during this time, and Mabel was very much in love. The couple welcomed two boys into the family when Mabel gave birth to John Ronald in January 1892, and Hilary Arthur in February 1894.

(Mis)adventures at Bank House

For the most part, life at Bank House was tolerable for the young Tolkien family. Arthur was in better health, and Mabel found new company when her sister May and brother-in-law Walter arrived on business about a year after John Ronald's birth. But living in a foreign country with small children proved to be a challenge for the Tolkiens as well. Venomous snakes lurked in the woodshed, and on one occasion, a neighbor's pet monkeys escaped onto the Tolkiens' property and chewed up some of the children's clothes.

At one point, when Tolkien was just beginning to walk, he was bitten by a baboon spider—a member of the tarantula family. Fortunately, he wasn't seriously harmed by the spider's venom, and he later recalled that he was too young to remember the incident: "I remember nothing about it, should not know it if I had not been told; and I do not dislike spiders particularly, and have no urge to kill them. I usually rescue those whom I find in the bath!"

Perhaps the most bizarre incident of his time in South Africa was when, as a baby, John Ronald Reuel Tolkien was kidnapped by a child! At the time, the family had a young servant named Isaak. Isaak, fascinated by baby Tolkien, took John Ronald out of Bank House and back to his village to show off to his family. The adventure wouldn't last long, though: Baby Tolkien was returned to Bank House the following day. According to Tolkien scholar Humphrey Carpenter, the incident was very upsetting to the Tolkien family, but Isaak wasn't fired. The family didn't believe he had any ill intentions; he was simply in awe of the baby and wanted to show him off.

THE MORE YOU KNOW

Years later, Isaak would go on to include Tolkien in his own child's name: Isaak Mister Tolkien Victor.

As with the baboon spider incident, Tolkien didn't remember the kidnapping. In fact, very little of his time in South Africa remained with him as he grew older. He, his mother, and his brother would leave the country just a few years later.

Childhood Days in England

John Ronald (or just Ronald to his friends) and his brother, Hilary, spent just a few years at Bank House in South Africa. In 1895, when Tolkien was three, he traveled with his mother and brother to England. It was intended to be just a visit with family. The young Tolkien even dictated a letter to his father about how he looked forward to returning to South Africa. However, his letter was never sent: On February 15, 1896, the day after young Tolkien dictated the letter to a nurse who wrote it for him, his father died of rheumatic fever. Father to the Father of Modern Fantasy, Arthur Tolkien was buried at the President Brand Cemetery in Bloemfontein, South Africa.

Left without an income, Mabel and her sons stayed in different parts of Birmingham—first at Mabel's parents' house, then at a cottage at Sarehole. To see the area around Sarehole Mill in person is to see the Shire; these rolling hills on the outskirts of Birmingham became a beloved part of young Tolkien's life and part of the inspiration for Hobbiton. As a boy, Tolkien would spend hours fishing in the nearby streams or hunting for bugs in the grass. Occasionally, he was chased out of the Sarehole Mill by the miller, George Andrew (nicknamed "The White Ogre" by the Tolkien brothers because of the white flour he often had on his face). This White Ogre would go on to inspire a small part of Middle-earth: the Old Mill of the Shire and the Shire's own ill-mannered miller, Ted Sandyman.

THE MORE YOU KNOW

As with much in those days, most of the information regarding Tolkien's early life is lost to time. What is known has been passed down through the years from Tolkien's own recollections as well as from those who knew him, though very few of Tolkien's childhood friends made it to adulthood: Most died in World War I. It was only after he became a well-known author and his life was thrust into the spotlight that people started to look deeper into his early years.

Catholicism in the Tolkien Home

J.R.R. Tolkien was a devout Roman Catholic from his early childhood, and Christian themes are central to most of the stories about Middle-earth. However, Tolkien himself was baptized as an infant in South Africa into the Anglican Church at the Cathedral of St. Andrew and St. Michael. It wasn't until he was eight years old that his mother converted to Catholicism and raised her sons in the Catholic Church, much to the displeasure of her family. Toward the end of his life, Tolkien wrote in a letter to his son, Michael, that even sixty years after her passing, he still considered his mother a quintessential part of his faith.

THE MORE YOU KNOW

Mabel Tolkien's conversion left a rift in her family. Her father had been raised in the Methodist Church and by the year 1900 was a devout Unitarian.

In a letter to Father Robert Murray in December 1953, Tolkien described The Lord of the Rings as a "fundamentally religious and Catholic work; unconsciously so at first but consciously in the revision." (And there were *many* revisions—but more on that later!) One primary example of the Roman Catholic faith in Tolkien's texts is the battle of the god of his legendarium, Eru Ilúvatar, against the evil Melkor, which parallels the struggles of God versus Satan in the Catholic Bible. Additionally, in many medieval traditions, the date of the crucifixion of Jesus is March 25, which also happens to be the day the One Ring is destroyed in the fires of Mount Doom.

After his mother's death when he was twelve (more on this later), Tolkien's faith would continue to be nurtured by the teachings of Father Francis Morgan. Referring to Morgan as a kind of second father, Tolkien would find his life and beliefs deeply shaped by this relationship.

The Middle-earth Afterlife

As a devout Catholic, Tolkien believed in a heaven, purgatory, and hell in adherence to Catholic teachings, and this is mirrored in his works. In his writings, the origins of the different people of Middle-earth dictate the "afterlife" they will be a part of when they die. For elves, the fulfillment of their being is to enter a kind of purgatory after death. In Tolkien's universe, this almost-purgatory is a real place known as the Halls of Mandos on the northernmost shores of the Undying Lands. The spirits of elves gather there to await their reincarnation. After a time, they will return to the physical world in a new body

The dwarves, meanwhile, were not made by the god of Tolkien's legendarium, Eru Ilúvatar, and were instead created by Aulë, one of the more powerful angelic beings, or Valar, who govern the physical world of Middle-earth and the Undying Lands. Though the dwarves do not know the details of their afterlife in the same way the elves know theirs, they believe that the Valar have a special place set aside for them in the Halls of Mandos.

The uncertainty about the afterlife of the humans of Middle-earth is critical to the themes of Tolkien. Unlike the elves, the humans have no idea what happens to them when they die, and that mystery is a terrifying thing to face for many in Middle-earth—so much so that in the Second Age, some even rebelled against the idea of death. At the heart of their fear of death was the twisted and corrupted Sauron, a Satan-like character. In Middle-earth lore, the humans on the island of Númenor in the Second Age were tricked by Sauron into believing immortality could be theirs if only they could take it from the Valar. But this was a lie, for even Sauron did not know where the souls of humans went when they died. Death for humans in Tolkien's Middle-earth is known as "the Gift of Men." What makes it a gift? In a world of immortal beings or creatures that live hundreds of years beyond their own lives, humans are motivated by their short lives to create their own destinies. They are encouraged to embrace death as a gift that not everyone in Middle-earth receives.

The More You Know

Though religion is a major theme in Tolkien's writing and life, it was not always at the forefront of his mind. In his letters, Tolkien recalled a period of about a decade from 1920 to the 1930s when his religious practice all but ceased for unknown reasons.

From The Silmarillion, "The Akallabêth"

The Eldar, you say, are unpunished, and even those who rebelled do not die. Yet that is to them neither reward nor punishment, but the fulfilment of their being. They cannot escape, and are bound to this world, never to leave it so long as it lasts, for its life is theirs.

Orphaned Brothers

After spending four years in Sarehole, the Tolkien family continued to move around Birmingham a few more times. (This was in large part due to Tolkien's schooling and their financial struggles.) In the autumn of 1900, Tolkien began attending school at King Edward's School as a fee-paying student. The family then moved to a house at 214 Alcester Road, Mosely, to be closer to the train that took Tolkien into the city for school. But financial struggles made him unable to attend his second term. A year later, the family was living in a home on Westfield Road in King's Heath. Then again in 1902, they moved to a house on Oliver Road, Edgbaston. The boys were enrolled at St. Phillip's Grammar school at this time, but Tolkien didn't stay at this school for long. He returned to King Edward's on scholarship in 1903.

Tolkien's young life would be met by tragedy yet again when his mother, Mabel, passed away on November 14, 1904, at the age of thirty-four. John Ronald was only twelve years old with a younger brother to care for. Mabel had been diagnosed with Type 1 diabetes earlier that year (seventeen years before Frederick Banting and Charles Best discovered how to isolate insulin to treat the disease). She briefly recovered enough to be discharged from the hospital, but fell into a diabetic coma from which she would not awaken.

Throughout his life, Tolkien spoke about his mother with deep love and affection. In addition to instilling in him his deep Catholic faith, he credited her with his love of languages and drawing.

LITERARY CONNECTIONS

Mabel Tolkien's death would have a profound impact on J.R.R. Tolkien's entire life as well as spill onto the pages of his stories. In The Lord of the Rings, the Ring-bearer Frodo Baggins is himself an orphan. He lost both parents at the age of twelve when they drowned in a boating accident. Frodo was then adopted by his second cousin, Bilbo, who he referred to as his uncle.

Father Francis Morgan

It was Father Francis Morgan, a Catholic priest from Wales, who became the Tolkien brothers' legal guardian when Mabel died. Morgan had met Mabel and her two young sons soon after Mabel converted to Catholicism, and he would often perform the weekly Catholic Mass at the oratory the Tolkien family attended. By Tolkien's own accounts, he and Father Morgan had a rather challenging relationship throughout most of his childhood. Tolkien recalled being very grateful for Morgan's taking him and his brother in, but also noted a strictness to Morgan and a formality to the relationship. Tolkien described Morgan as "very military."

In one letter to his son Michael, he wrote that Morgan "was an upper-class Welsh-Spaniard Tory, and seemed to some just a pottering old gossip. He was—and he was not. I first learned charity and forgiveness from him; and in the light of it pierced even the 'liberal' darkness out of which I came, knowing more about 'Bloody Mary' than the Mother of Jesus." The situation with Father Morgan was made even more tense when, at the age of sixteen, J.R.R. Tolkien met the woman who would eventually become his wife, Edith Mary Bratt. At the time, Tolkien was living as a boarder with a woman named Louise Faulkner, who was also housing Edith.

Father Morgan did not think well of this relationship, believing that Edith would be a distraction to the young Tolkien's studies, and he forbade Tolkien from associating with her at all until he turned twenty-one years old.

Tolkien later wrote about the experience: "Trouble arose: and I had to choose between disobeying and grieving (or deceiving) a guardian who had been a father to me, more than most real fathers, but without any obligation, and 'dropping' the love-affair until I was 21." Despite his fondness for Edith, Tolkien chose to obey Father Morgan and would spend the next three years not seeing or writing to Edith at all. Though Tolkien claimed that he did not regret his decision, he did recall that it was one of the most challenging times of his young life. Fortunately, it wouldn't be the end for their relationship (more on this later!).

LITERARY CONNECTIONS

Just as Father Morgan served as a mentor and father figure for Tolkien after his mother's death, the wizard Gandalf played a guiding, parental role for Frodo in *The Lord of the Rings.* In early drafts of *The Hobbit,* however, Gandalf was going to be named Bladorthin. Though it is never directly translated in Tolkien's work, a rough meaning can be derived from the element *Blador,* meaning "wide open country," and *thin,* meaning "grey." So the name translates roughly to "the Grey Country."

The Immortal Four

Alongside J.R.R. Tolkien during his studies at King Edward's School were three young men who would eventually form the Tea Club and Barrovian Society—better known as the TCBS. Started in the summer term of 1911, this literary and debating club at King Edward's would be the basis of Tolkien's other friendships throughout the rest of his life.

The club included Robert Gilson, poet Geoffrey Blanche Smith (called G.B.), and Christopher Wiseman. Together with Tolkien, they were the founding members of the TCBS and would later come to be known as the Immortal Four. These close friends led discussions on everything they'd been reading, from poetry to prose. They also acted as an editing group of sorts, giving each other feedback and ideas to further flesh out the creative writing project(s) each member was working on. The TCBS even contributed to Tolkien's development of his Elvish language (more on that later). Several other members would occasionally join, but these four young men steadfastly remained the constant.

The group stayed in touch after leaving school in 1914, and they met one final time on September 25, 1915, in

Lichfield, as World War I loomed. While all four young men would later enlist in the war, only Tolkien and Wiseman would return.

LITERARY CONNECTIONS

The bond that Tolkien formed with his friends in the TCBS has strong parallels with the bond linking the Fellowship of the Ring's members. In addition, the deep sadness of losing his friends in the war would permeate his writing, where themes of both loss and sacrifice frequent the pages of his stories.

Elvish Script

During the time that Tolkien was discussing books and cultivating a love of poetry with the TCBS, he was also putting the love of languages he'd inherited from his mother to use. It was around 1910–1911 that he started to create the first of many fictional languages for his stories: Elvish. (Originally it was called Gnomish, as Tolkien first called his elves gnomes.) J.R.R. Tolkien's Elvish language is one of the most detailed and complicated in all of fantasy literature!

To fully understand his construction of languages, it's important to note that Tolkien constructed his stories around his fictional languages not the other way around. First he made the language, then he made the characters to say the words he had created. Elvish was originally based on the languages of Finnish and Welsh: Finnish for the Quenya form of Elvish, a language associated with the High Elves, and Welsh for Sindarin, the language of the Grey Elves of Beleriand. (Sindarin is the Elvish language most spoken throughout The Lord of the Rings books as well as the Peter Jackson film trilogy and *The Rings of Power* television show.) Tolkien also utilized his love of both Latin and Greek for the more classical or older-feeling features of his languages.

Sindarin Elvish would make its way into the other cultures of Middle-earth as well: Frodo Baggins guesses the riddle to enter Moria by knowing the Elvish word for "friend." Elvish has even made its way into the real world. Today, there are dozens of websites, books, and online communities that teach fans how to speak Elvish. David Salo, the man responsible for helping construct the Elvish language for Peter Jackson's Lord of the Rings trilogy, has even published a book of over 450 pages called *A Gateway to Sindarin* that provides a detailed linguistic analysis of the Elvish language.

THE MORE YOU KNOW

Elvish has gained notoriety in tattoo form. Eight of the nine cast members in *The Fellowship of the Ring*'s fellowship were each tattooed with the number nine in the Tengwar script while they filmed the movies. (John Rhys-Davies, the actor who plays Gimli the dwarf, declined to be tattooed and instead sent his stunt double, Brett Beattie, in his place.) Additionally, former Atlético Madrid football stars Fernando Torres and Sergio Agüero have tattoos of their names in Elvish script.

As influenced by Tolkien, the use of constructed languages continues to be a staple of both the fantasy and the science fiction genres. Two different languages were created for the television adaptation of George R.R. Martin's best-selling series A Song of Ice and Fire; Richard Adams created the animal language Lapine in his novel *Watership Down*;

and the language of the Na'vi was created for the film *Avatar,* directed by James Cameron. One notable constructed language that wasn't influenced by Tolkien was Klingon in the Star Trek franchise. The creator of the Klingon language, Marc Okrand, said any influence was unintentional, and he instead drew inspiration from the Indigenous languages of America and Southeast Asia.

From The Fellowship of the Ring ("Namárië," or "Galadriel's Lament in Lórien")

Ai! laurië lantar lassi súrinen,
yéni únótimë ve rámar aldaron!
Yéni ve lintë yuldar avánier
mi oromardi lisse-miruvóreva
Andúnë pella, Vardo tellumar
nu luini yassen tintilar i eleni
ómaryo airetári-lírinen.

. . . ar hísië
untúpa Calaciryo míri oialë.
Sí vanwa ná, Rómello vanwa, Valimar!

Namárië! Nai hiruvalyë Valimar!
Nai elyë hiruva! Namárië!

Translation:

Ah! like gold fall the leaves in the wind,
long years numberless as the wings of trees!
The years have passed like swift draughts
of the sweet mead in lofty halls beyond the West,
beneath the blue vaults of Varda
wherein the stars tremble in the song of her voice, holy
and queenly.

. . . and mist
covers the jewels of Calacirya for ever.
Now lost, lost for those from the East is Valimar!

Farewell! Maybe thou shalt find Valimar.
Maybe even thou shalt find it. Farewell!

Switzerland

A real-life adventure with Tolkien's brother, Hilary, inspired Bilbo's journey through the Misty Mountains in *The Hobbit*! The year was 1911 and Tolkien, then nineteen years old, and Hilary joined a trek of twelve people through the Swiss Alps over the summer. The group hiked from Interlaken to Lauterbrunnen, which was around 7½ miles on foot, then camped near Mürren. Tolkien recalled, "We slept rough—the men-folk—often in hayloft of cowbyre, since we were walking by map and avoided roads and never booked [a place to stay]."

Lauterbrunnen is a picturesque Swiss village in a valley with stunning views of steep cliffs as well as several glaciers and seventy-two different waterfalls. For Tolkien, it would be the inspiration for the secluded elven kingdom of Rivendell. The hike through Kleine Scheidegg Pass and Grimsel Pass in Lauterbrunnen was the basis of Bilbo's adventure through the passes of the Misty Mountains.

The real-life trip, much like Bilbo's fictional one, proved dangerous. Though there were no stone giants in the real valley, Tolkien came close to being seriously injured or even worse. In a letter to his son Michael, he recalled that the weather that year was unseasonably hot and had melted a decent portion of snow in the Alps, loosening many of the boulders. In one particular area, boulders suddenly tumbled down the surrounding mountains: "anything from the size of oranges to large footballs, and a few much larger. They were whizzing across our path and plunging into the ravine . . . a large lump of rock shot between us. About a foot at most before my unmanly knees." Fortunately, Tolkien and his brother were able to avoid the boulders, and it was a trip Tolkien looked back on fondly. In his letter, he wrote that he was sad to leave the views of the snowy valley.

LITERARY CONNECTION

While not in The Lord of the Rings trilogy, Thranduil, the king of the elves of Mirkwood and father to Legolas, is a character in *The Hobbit* book. Though he was not given a name in the book. Tolkien referred to him as "the Elvenking." It was only after he wrote *The Hobbit* that he gave this Elvenking a name and back-story.

"A Very Simple Sense of Humor"

After his summer trip to Switzerland, Tolkien enrolled in Oxford University in the fall of 1911. Initially studying classics, he later changed his degree to English language and literature.

Despite the losses he'd endured in his young life, Tolkien had a reputation for being a jokester. A fan of the Marx Brothers, he described himself once as having "a very simple sense of humor (which even my appreciative critics find tiresome)." Humphrey Carpenter's biography of Tolkien tells one story of a New Year's Eve party in which Tolkien dressed up as a polar bear by draping a sheepskin rug over himself and painting his face white. It wasn't even a costume party; he did it just for the fun of it! In another instance, Tolkien supposedly dressed up as an Anglo-Saxon warrior and chased a neighbor down the road with an axe—though there are few details about this particular prank.

LITERARY CONNECTIONS

Tolkien's jokester nature carried over into his works, most notably through the characters of Merry and Pippin in The Lord of the Rings. The simple humor of the two hobbits serves as a foil for the more serious themes and plot points throughout the novels.

Tolkien was such a skilled prankster that he and a friend once stole a bus and drove it around picking up other Oxford students. He later recalled: "Geoffrey and I 'captured' a bus and drove it up to Cornmarket making various unearthly noises followed by a mad crowd of mingled varsity and 'townese.' It was chock full of undergrads before it reached the Carfax. There I addressed a few stirring words to a huge mob before descending. . . . There were no disciplinary consequences of all this!"

Although he would experience loss through the deaths of his parents, two World Wars, and into later life, Tolkien kept his "very simple sense of humor." A prankster even in his elder years, he was known to offer up his false teeth as payment to store cashiers who weren't paying attention.

When Pen Met Paper

During his third year at Oxford, on September 24, 1914, twenty-two-year-old Tolkien wrote the poem "The Voyage of Éarendel the Evening Star." This poem is thought to be the first words he ever wrote about his fantasy world, Middle-earth. It tells the story of the half-elf, half-human Eärendil (also styled Éarendel or Eärendel), who is trying to escape the "gloom of the mid-world's rim" (Middle-earth, which is currently at war). Eärendil sails to the Undying Lands to try to convince angelic beings known as the Valar to help defeat the evil dark lord, Morgoth, who is responsible for the war.

"The Voyage of Éarendel the Evening Star" is believed to set the stage for what would eventually become *The Book of Lost Tales* and the rest of the world of Eä (the universe within which Middle-earth is a continent on the planet Arda).

LITERARY CONNECTIONS

The name Eärendil comes from the Anglo-Saxon word *éarendel,* which is associated with the star Rigel. Rigel is an important star in navigation, as it is the brightest of the Orion constellation (making it a fitting inspiration for Eärendil, the seafaring half-elf and half-human voyager in Tolkien's poem).

Tolkien was very much alone in the gloom of it all at the time he wrote these first words about Middle-earth. Many of his friends from the TCBS, as well as his brother, Hilary, and other young men in his circle, had already enlisted to fight in World War I. John Garth, Tolkien scholar and author of *Tolkien and the Great War*, noted that things like fear, resourcefulness, sadness, courage, and seemingly hopeless odds were all experienced by Tolkien during the war and became themes he wove into his writing.

The story of Eärendil wouldn't be read by the public until after Tolkien's death. It was first published in *The Silmarillion* by Tolkien's son, Christopher, in 1977 (more on this later). In *The Silmarillion*, readers learn Eärendil is the father of Elrond, the half-elf ruler in The Lord of the Rings. Even more details of Eärendil's story would be revealed in 1984, when Christopher released the second volume of *The Book of Lost Tales*, which featured a chapter called "The Tale of Eärendel."

From "The Voyage of Éarendel the Evening Star"

Éarendel sprang up from the Ocean's cup
In the gloom of the mid-world's rim;
From the door of Night as a ray of light
Leapt over the twilight brim,
And launching his bark like a silver spark
From the golden-fading sand;
Down the sunlit breath of Day's fiery Death
He sped from Westerland.

He threaded his path o'er the aftermath
of the splendour of the Sun,
and wandered far past many a star
in his gleaming galleon.
On the gathering tide of darkness ride
the argosies of the sky,
and spangle the night with their sails of light
as the streaming star goes by.

Unheeding he dips past these twinkling ships,
by his wayward spirit whirled
on an endless quest through the darkling West
o'er the margin of the world;
and he fares in haste o'er the jewelled waste
and the dusk from whence he came
with his heart afire with bright desire
and his face in silver flame.

A Long-Expected War

Also known as the Great War, World War I officially began in 1914, while Tolkien was studying at Oxford. Less than a year later, after finishing his degree, he enlisted in the army in July 1915. Having graduated with First Class Honors, Tolkien obtained a commission in the British Army as a second lieutenant and trained in Staffordshire, England, for eleven months. He was then summoned to France, where he would spend five months serving as a signals officer on the front lines, including at the Battle of the Somme (more on this later).

Throughout the war, the TCBS maintained a correspondence as well as a steadfast friendship. As member G.B. Smith wrote in one letter, "[T]he death of one of its members cannot, I am determined, dissolve the TCBS. . . . Death can make us loathsome and helpless as individuals, but it cannot put an end to the immortal four!"

But it was here that Tolkien's life would yet again be marred by loss. Both G.B. Smith and Robert Gilson were killed in action during the war. The other remaining Immortal Four member, Christopher Wiseman, would receive a hand injury in 1917 during his time in the Royal Navy, but he survived the Great War—the only one of Tolkien's closest friends to come out of the conflict alive. The loss of Gilson and Smith would cement Tolkien and Wiseman's friendship for the rest of their lives, and they continued to send each other letters up until Tolkien's passing. One of Tolkien's final letters to Wiseman (written just a few months after his eighty-first birthday) was signed "your most devoted friend." The letter discussed Tolkien's recent health troubles and also how he had been put on a more restrictive diet. He was especially annoyed at being unable to drink any wine.

THE MORE YOU KNOW

Christopher Luke Wiseman, Tolkien's longtime friend from the TCBS, became the headmaster of Queens College after serving in the war. He lived to be almost one hundred years old, passing away in 1987 at the age of ninety four. Tolkien would name his son Christopher after Wiseman.

Reuniting with Edith

Ever the scholar, Tolkien had been concerned he wouldn't be able to finish his degree at Oxford before fighting in the war. Luckily, he had found a loophole: There was a way for him to train with the army while at university and delay his call to the front lines until he had taken the end-of-year exams. He passed the exams in June 1915. Tolkien, graduate-turned-soldier, moved to a new house, grew a mustache, and bought a motorcycle—which he used on weekends to go see Edith.

Indeed, in 1913, three years after Father Francis Morgan had forbidden Tolkien's relationship with Edith Bratt, the two had reunited! Keeping his promise to Morgan to not contact Edith until he turned twenty-one, Tolkien wrote her a letter on his birthday. In his letter, Tolkien explained that he had never stopped loving her in the years they hadn't spoken. Unfortunately, at the time of his letter, Edith was engaged to a friend of her brother, a man named George Field. In her reply, she told Tolkien that she had only agreed to marry Field because she wasn't sure whether Tolkien still loved her. He did.

On January 8, 1913, just five days after his twenty-first birthday, Tolkien traveled to Cheltenham where Edith was living with a family friend. By the end of the day, Tolkien had proposed and Edith had accepted. The two would be married on March 22, 1916, just a few months before he left for France and the front lines.

THE MORE YOU KNOW

Two of Tolkien's sons served as soldiers in the British Armed Forces during World War II, which deeply affected him. Several of the letters that Tolkien wrote revolve around the war. In 1944, he wrote his son Christopher, "I sometimes feel appalled at the thought of the sum total of human misery all over the world at the present moment: the millions parted, fretting, wasting in unprofitable days—quite apart from torture, pain, death, bereavement, injustice. . . . All we do know, and that to a large extend by direct experience, is that evil labours with vast power and perpetual success."

Somewhere in France Covered in Mud

The Battle of the Somme, which raged from July until November of 1916, was one of the bloodiest battles in the history of warfare at the time, and J.R.R. Tolkien lived through it. For those five months, the British and French armies attempted to occupy enemy territory on both sides of the now famous river Somme. An estimated 3 million people fought in the battle, and most historians estimate that more than 1 million were either wounded or killed in action. Both the British and the German armies each lost an estimated 400,000 troops. On the first day alone, the British Army sustained some 57,000 casualties.

The More You Know

It was during the Battle of the Somme that J.R.R. Tolkien's friends Robert Gilson and G.B. Smith were killed. Gilson died on the first day of combat, July 1, 1916. Smith died in a field hospital on December 3, four days after being wounded in the battle.

Finding himself right in the middle of one of the deadliest events in history, Tolkien was just twenty-three years old when he fought in the Battle of the Somme. The experience would stay with him for the rest of his life. The constant threat of death combined with the coming winter, as well as the rats and illnesses that ran rampant through the battalions on the front lines, created what Tolkien called a "nightmare." It also inspired the landscapes of Mordor and the Dead Marshes in The Lord of the Rings. The camaraderie Tolkien experienced with other soldiers in the trenches parallels the bonds between the members in the Fellowship of the Ring.

Although many books present a valiant image of soldiers sacrificing themselves for the good of the many, Tolkien wouldn't write the battles against the forces of Mordor as glorious or honorable. For Tolkien, war was destructive and took the lives of many of his friends. Years later, he would write in a letter to his son Michael when Michael became an officer cadet at the Royal Military College in Sandhurst that "One War is enough for any man. I hope you will be spared a second. Either the bitterness of youth or that of middle-age is enough for a life-time: both is too much."

In the midst of the Battle of the Somme, Tolkien's thoughts kept returning to the story forming in his head. The seeds of the fictional world of Middle-earth were being planted.

The Return Journey

While fighting in the Battle of the Somme, Tolkien came down with trench fever. First identified during the war, trench fever is an infectious disease that can cause severe fever and headaches, leg pain, muscle aches, and rash. In poor health, Tolkien first went to a field hospital, then was sent back to England to recover at several hospitals and homes. Due to his ongoing illness and general health struggles, Tolkien never returned to the front lines. Instead, he would sporadically work garrison duties when he was well enough.

His time on the front lines took a toll on Tolkien's psyche. On top of his physical battle with trench fever, Tolkien's experiences at the Battle of the Somme triggered a mental shift that would stay with him his whole life. He wrote in a letter to writer W.H. Auden: "I can honestly say that I have not been able to shake off the effects of the war . . . it left me with a sense of disgust, and a conviction that such a thing should never happen again." Two of the other three members of the TCBS were dead, and the third, Christopher Wiseman, was injured. Tolkien's battalion, the 11th Lancashire Fusiliers, lost so many troops that it was eventually disbanded.

The third book in The Lord of the Rings trilogy, *The Return of the King*, features a chapter in which the hobbits return to the Shire after their harrowing journey. The scene pays homage to combat veterans like Tolkien himself who returned to a world they no longer recognized. Just as Frodo struggled with transitioning back to the peaceful life with his fellow hobbits, Tolkien had to return to England and "normalcy" after fighting in World War I. As the Warden of the Houses of Healing says in *The Return of the King*: "[T]he world is full enough of hurts and mischances without wars to multiply them."

THE MORE YOU KNOW

As Tolkien fought on the front lines, almost 2,000 miles east in the Russian Empire, one of the first female soldiers was also fighting. Maria Bochkareva, with the help of her commander, wrote to Tsar Nicholas II requesting his permission to fight alongside the men. The Tsar consented. Bochkareva saw front-line duties with the 5th Corps, 28th Regiment of the Second Army. During the February Revolution in 1917, she was given special dispensation to form a 2,000-women volunteer unit within the army. It was called the 1st Russian Women's Battalion of Death.

Samwise the Brave

Who would a reader of fantasy literature trust to save the world if it were in peril? Perhaps a lost king who heroically united two kingdoms? Or maybe a powerful wizard able to hurl fireballs and cast out evil from the souls of kings? For J.R.R. Tolkien, it was neither. He decided to give the responsibility of saving the world to hobbits.

One of these heroic hobbits, the gardener Samwise Gamgee, is based on a specific kind of soldier that J.R.R. Tolkien fought alongside during World War I: a batman. Sometimes called an orderly, a batman was a soldier assigned to a commissioned officer as a personal servant. As a batman, this soldier would do everything from passing orders along from the officer to his troops, to maintaining the officer's uniform, to acting as a bodyguard for him during combat. Although not nearly as well-known as their commanding officers, these men serving on the front lines of World War I inspired the fan-favorite hobbit.

Mirroring the World War I batman role, Samwise shows deference to Frodo, referring to him as "Mister Frodo" and even sometimes "Master." He acts as a servant to the Ring-bearer, cooking for him, carrying his baggage, and, at a pivotal moment of great peril, physically carrying Frodo on his back up the slopes of Mount Doom.

While Sam is the Tolkienian embodiment of the English batman, he is also considered by some scholars to be the Alfred Pennyworth to Frodo's Bruce Wayne (aka Batman). The two characters form a strong bond throughout The Lord of the Rings series, and Sam even vows to return to his (apparently) dead master in *The Two Towers*, to be reunited with Frodo in death.

The More You Know

In order to prepare for the role of Samwise Gamgee, actor Sean Astin gained 35–40 pounds. He also managed to get his daughter, Alexandra, a role in Peter Jackson's film of *The Return of the King*. Alexandra plays Samwise Gamgee's daughter, Elanor.

The Book of Lost Tales

It was during his time recovering from the war that J.R.R. Tolkien began to write *The Book of Lost Tales.* Started in 1917 as a collection of stories set in Middle-earth, *The Book of Lost Tales* consists of vignettes that give readers a glimpse into that world. Though he never fully completed any of the tales while he lived, they formed the backstory to what would eventually become The Lord of the Rings. Split into two volumes, *The Book of Lost Tales* takes after religious texts like the Bible and the Quran, with stories describing the creation of the universe, the god and angelic beings involved in that creation, and the many wars fought by the elves, dwarves, and humans against evil.

The stories in *The Book of Lost Tales* were the earliest forms of the complex myths Tolkien later wove into his magnum opus, *The Silmarillion,* and the two volumes themselves would eventually become the first two parts of his son Christopher's own life's work: a twelve-volume series known as The History of Middle-earth. (More on these works later.)

Literary Connections

While the stories in the two volumes of *The Book of Lost Tales* recount a history similar to that chronicled in the stories found in *The Silmarillion*, they are written in a less formal style and often depict different interactions with the various elven cultures explored in *The Silmarillion*.

Tolkien wrote *The Book of Lost Tales* in Great Haywood, a village in Staffordshire, where he spent part of his recovery after the Battle of the Somme. Sixty-six years later (and ten years after Tolkien's death), in 1983, the first volume was published. The second volume followed in 1984.

Tevildo and Other Talking Animals

One of Middle-earth's greatest villains, the Dark Lord Sauron, started off somewhat fluffier than in his final form! In *The Book of Lost Tales*, the Sauron-like antagonist is a talking cat named Tevildo, the Prince of Cats. Serving as the primary villain of one of Tolkien's most epic stories of Middle-earth, the tale of Beren and Lúthien, Tevildo is "possessed of an evil sprite," as *The Book of Lost Tales* explains.

Titled "The Tale of Tinúviel" in an earlier version, this story follows the characters Beren and Lúthien on an epic quest to seize a sacred jewel called a Silmaril from the crown of the evil lord Morgoth so the two can marry. Along the way, they are captured by Tevildo. With the help of their talking dog, Huan, Beren and Lúthien eventually escape the clutches of the giant cat. Tevildo was scrapped from later drafts and replaced with another villain, named Thû, the Lord of Werewolves. Thû was also eventually replaced, this time by a character from *The Hobbit*: the Necromancer. Finally, the necromancer would become Sauron, the titular Lord of the Rings.

The recurring theme of talking animals throughout Middle-earth shifted a few times as Tolkien took a much more serious approach to his legendarium. The talking trolls of *The Hobbit* were replaced by the fearsome cave-trolls of The Lord of the Rings. However, readers can still find a few talking animals scattered throughout Middle-earth. Notably, a talking spider gives Bilbo's sword, Sting, its namesake.

LITERARY CONNECTIONS

Thought by some to be a holdover from Tolkien's experience writing *The Hobbit* for children is a brief inner monologue of a fox early on in *The Fellowship of the Ring*. The fox comments on how strange it is to come across hobbits sleeping outdoors. This fox is never seen or heard from again in the trilogy.

More character shifts are found between Tolkien's earlier writings of Middle-earth and his later works. The Lord of the Rings character who would one day become Aragorn, son of Arathorn, heir to the throne of Gondor and uniter of the two realms, was originally a hobbit called Trotter. Much like Aragorn, Trotter was initially set to guide Frodo and the rest of the hobbits from the human city of Bree to the elven land of Rivendell (also called *Imladris* in Elvish). Trotter was also a wandering ranger and a good friend of Gandalf the Grey. He earned the name Trotter because he wore wooden shoes: The sound of his footsteps was said to be like the sound of a horse's hooves!

The Real-Life Beren and Lúthien

Those who knew them recalled Tolkien and his wife as being very much in love. Friend and fellow author C.S. Lewis described Tolkien as "the most married man I know." Their romance had survived a disapproving guardian and years apart—and even served as the inspiration for one of Middle-earth's most famous couples, Beren and Lúthien.

In addition to their encounter with Tevildo, Prince of Cats, Beren and Lúthien appear in several of Tolkien's stories, not just in *The Book of Lost Tales* but also in *The Silmarillion,* and are briefly mentioned in The Lord of the Rings. In Middle-earth lore, Lúthien Tinuviel is the elven princess the human Beren falls in love with. Lúthien's father, the elven King Thingol, opposes their union, demanding Beren prove himself by obtaining a sacred jewel called a Silmaril from the evil Morgoth. The two face many dangers on the road to acquire this jewel, and most of the companions they meet along the way perish. When Beren's injuries during their escape from the villain Morgoth prove fatal, Lúthien journeys to the elven purgatory, Halls of Mandos, to plead for a second opportunity at life for Beren.

In the tale, Beren first falls for Lúthien when he sees her dancing in a glade of hemlocks. This detail was taken directly from Tolkien's own romance: One night in 1917, he watched Edith dance in a hemlock glade, and was inspired to write the story of the elf and human lovers. As Tolkien recalled: "[S]he was the source of the story that in time became the chief part of the *Silmarillion*. It was first conceived in a small woodland glade filled with hemlocks at Roos in Yorkshire (where I was for a brief time in command of an outpost of the Humber Garrison in 1917, and she was able to live with me for a while). In those days her hair was raven, her skin clear, her eyes brighter than you have seen them, and she could sing—and *dance*."

The Tolkiens' love and their personal connection to the relationship between Beren and Lúthien is particularly evident on their shared gravestone in Wolvercote Cemetery in north Oxford. Etched in the marker where John Ronald and Edith Mary Tolkien rest are their names, their dates of birth and death, and two other names: Lúthien for Edith Mary, and Beren for John Ronald.

THE MORE YOU KNOW

After Edith passed in 1971, Tolkien referenced their personal connection to Beren and Lúthien, writing in a letter that Edith "was my Lúthien and I was her Beren. And now she is gone. And I am alone."

From The Silmarillion ("Of Beren and Lúthien")

Among the tales of sorrow and ruin that come down to us from the darkness of those days there are yet some in which amid weeping there is and under the shadow of death light that endures. And of those histories most fair still in the ears of the Elves is the tale of Beren and Lúthien.

. . . It is told in the Lay of Leithian that Beren came stumbling into Doriath grey and bowed as with many years of woe, so great had been the torment of the road. But wandering in the summer in the woods of Neldoreth he came upon Lúthien, daughter of Thingol and Melian, at a time of evening under moonrise, as she danced upon the unfading grass in the glades beside Esgalduin. Then all memory of his pain departed from him, and he fell into an enchantment; for Lúthien was the most beautiful of all the Children of Ilúvatar.

The Fall of Gondolin

Another tale J.R.R. Tolkien first drafted in his *Book of Lost Tales* while recovering from war tells the story of the fall of Gondolin. This story would eventually become a cornerstone for *The Silmarillion* and is the first tale he ever wrote for his eventual legendarium.

The Fall of Gondolin tells the tale of a hidden elven city that fights and ultimately loses in a battle against the ultimate evil of the First Age, Sauron's master, Morgoth. Shaping the story based on his own wartime experiences, Tolkien brought siege engines, mechanized warfare, and multiple dragons to reign down death and destruction on the elven kingdom in *The Fall of Gondolin,* all while countless soldiers were being lost to the war in the real world that was still going on in 1917.

The story would go through multiple iterations throughout Tolkien's life and even after his death, continuing to change from its initial writing through its publication in *The Silmarillion* and up until its stand-alone publication in 2018. However, one thing remained constant: the connection to the early poem about Eärendil that Tolkien read aloud to his friends at the Essay Club at Exeter College. Well received then by his friends and later by countless readers and Tolkien enthusiasts, the story became part of the backdrop for The Lord of the Rings trilogy.

LITERARY CONNECTIONS

In an announcement of the book-length publication of *The Fall of Gondolin,* Tolkien Society chair Shaun Gunner said that this work was essentially "the Holy Grail of Tolkien Texts" and was in line with *The Children of Húrin* and *Beren and Lúthien* as one of Tolkien's Great Tales.

Tolkien's Children

Edith Tolkien would give birth to four children between 1917 and 1929. The eldest, John Francis, was born in November 1917 and became an ordained Catholic priest in 1946. His middle name, Francis, was in honor of Father Francis Morgan, the legal guardian of Tolkien and his brother, Hilary, for several years. Their second child, Michael Hilary, born in October 1920, was named after J.R.R. Tolkien's younger brother. Michael served in the Royal Air Force during World War II as a flight lieutenant, and, after retiring from service, he became a schoolteacher.

LITERARY CONNECTIONS

Tolkien's novella *Roverandom* was created in an attempt to console young Michael, who had just lost his toy dog on the beach. Michael, as Tolkien's second son, is thought to be the "little boy Two" of the story. In the story, "little boy Two" loses his toy dog, Rover, at the beach, but is reunited with Rover when Rover becomes a real dog by the end of the story. Tolkien wrote the story based on his oral narrative and tried to have it published in 1937, but his publisher rejected it. *Roverandom* did not see publication until 1998.

J.R.R. and Edith's third child, Christopher John Reuel Tolkien, was born in November 1924. Like his brother Michael, he served as a member of the Royal Air Force during World War II. As will be explored later in more detail, Christopher would become deeply involved in his father's work, editing twenty-four manuscripts of his father's posthumously published works and creating the original maps for The Lord of the Rings trilogy.

Priscilla Mary Anne, the Tolkiens' fourth child and only daughter, was born in June 1929. A probation officer and social worker in her adult years, she later became very heavily involved in The Tolkien Society, even serving as its honorary vice president from 1986 until her death in 2022. The last of Tolkien's children to be born, Priscilla was also the last surviving child of J.R.R. Tolkien. Together with her oldest brother, John, Priscilla co-edited and published *The Tolkien Family Album* in 1992. The book shares photographs of Tolkien and his family, memorabilia, and other illustrations that offer a very personal look into the life of J.R.R. Tolkien.

The Dictionary Job

As fitting the creator of several languages, J.R.R. Tolkien spent some time after serving in World War I working to put together the *New English Dictionary*, or, as it would be later known, the *Oxford English Dictionary*. Started in 1878 and taken over by Oxford University after a number of mishaps, the dictionary was set to be complete in the early 1900s. But following the death of the original editor as well as the onset of World War I taking many young men away from England, the dictionary's authors needed new assistants.

In the fall of 1918, Tolkien took a job as an assistant lexicographer. He had been given the position by his former undergraduate tutor, William Craigie, who also gave Tolkien's family rooms at Oxford to live in at the time. Tolkien would spend the next eighteen months meticulously researching words, defining and sometimes creating more than one hundred words for the dictionary. He sorted through dozens of examples of the words being used throughout history. He spent most of his time on words that began with the letter "w," including "warm," "wasp," "water," "wick," and "winter."

The More You Know

The man who worked on the *Oxford English Dictionary* would eventually be mentioned in it as well! In the dictionary, "Tolkienian" is an adjective that means ""Of or pertaining to Tolkien or his works." The earliest found use is in 1954, in the writing of C.S. Lewis, one of J.R.R. Tolkien's dearest friends. "Tolkienian" was officially added to the *Oxford English Dictionary* in 1986, as part of *A Supplement to the Oxford English Dictionary*, Volume IV.

Tolkien loved working on the dictionary. He later said of the job, "I learned more in those two years than in any other equal period of my life." He even went on to note that he never understood why people would say that languages were dull, declaring that a new language to him was just like a new wine or sweet treat. The writer's love of language was bested only by the love he held for his wife and children.

Letters from Father Christmas

Just three days before Christmas, on December 22, 1920, when J.R.R. Tolkien's oldest child, John, was three and his second child, Michael, was only a few months old, a letter arrived at the Tolkien home. It was from Father Christmas! (Really, it was from Tolkien posing as the bearded man from the north.) As one of the ways Tolkien was known to dote on his family, it would be the first of many letters he wrote to his children from "Father Christmas." In fact, Tolkien would continue the holiday tradition for the next twenty-three years!

Each letter provides a glimpse into the fantastical imagination of J.R.R. Tolkien. The letters were mostly told from the perspective of Father Christmas about the adventures he'd had the previous year. But sometimes the letters were written by the elven secretary, Ilbereth, or a clumsy North Polar Bear known as the Great Polar Bear, who also featured prominently in many of the stories. Over the course of the letters, the Great Polar Bear accidentally destroys Father Christmas's home twice—once by collapsing a pole on the house in a failed attempt to get a Christmas hat and another by setting off fireworks. The Snowman gardener and a number of other fantastical creatures like elves and goblins also make appearances in Tolkien's Father Christmas letters.

These letters also include some of the first appearances of the Elvish letters written in the Tengwar script found in Middle-earth. (Though the language was called Arctic at the time Tolkien wrote the Father Christmas letters.) He also included his own colorful illustrations to accompany these letters.

The final six letters focused more on the real-world events affecting England at the time. The 1939 letter reflected an anxious Father Christmas: "I am very busy and things are very difficult this year owing to this horrible war. Many of my messages have never come back." Just three months before that Christmas, on September 1, 1939, Adolf Hitler's Nazi troops had fired the first shots of the Second World War. Britain and France declared war two days later.

THE MORE YOU KNOW

Starting on September 1, 1939, the British government began Operation Pied Piper, which saw the evacuation of nearly 1.5 million people (including hundreds of thousands of children) from urban centers like London, Manchester, and Glasgow to relocate them to the countryside. Many children returned home a few months later in January 1940. Though Tolkien's children were never evacuated, his close friend C.S. Lewis would later write about the evacuation in *The Lion, the Witch and The Wardrobe* (published in 1950).

The December 1940 letter was not much different from the one from 1939. Father Christmas remarks that he continues to have a difficult time preparing for Christmas: "This horrible war is reducing all our stocks, and in so many countries children are living far from their homes." The letters from 1941 and 1942 detail an even worse situation, as Tolkien wrote in somewhat more detail about a war happening in the North Pole against the goblins.

Tolkien wrote his final letter from Father Christmas in 1943. Addressed to his daughter Priscilla, Tolkien wrote: "I suppose you will be hanging up your stocking just once more. . . . After this I shall have to say goodbye more or less. . . . We always keep the old numbers of our friends and their letters; and later on we hope to come back when they are grown up and have houses of their own and children." All twenty-three Father Christmas letters were published after Tolkien's death by his son Christopher in a book called *The Father Christmas Letters.*

A Letter from Father Christmas, 1920

Dear John,

I heard you ask today what I was like & where I lived. I have drawn ME & My House for you. Take care of the picture. I am just off now for Oxford with my bundle of toys—some for you.

Hope I shall arrive in time: the snow is very thick at the North Pole tonight:

Yr loving Fr. Chr.

The Unexpected Interview

Just months before J.R.R. Tolkien's Father Christmas first wrote to the Tolkien home, the course of the author's life drastically changed. It was the summer of 1920, and he had recently applied to be a Reader (similar to an associate professor position) in English language at the University of Leeds in England. The interview went so well he later remarked, "I knew privately before I left Leeds that I had got the job."

As a Reader, Tolkien was responsible for occasionally lecturing on Old English or philology, and also conducting research. When he wasn't constructing an entire coursework on Anglo-Saxon and Middle English, Tolkien was running home to be with his family on the weekends. Indeed, his second child, Michael, was born just after the start of the new term, in October 1920. Around this time, Tolkien was also offered a job in Cape Town, South Africa. While it was an opportunity to return to his birth country, he refused the offer in order to stay with his wife and sons. Instead, he continued his role as Reader at Leeds.

LITERARY CONNECTIONS

The University of Leeds houses a special Blue Plaque—one of many placed around England to commemorate places that made a significant contribution to Tolkien's life and works.

E.V. Gordon

In 1922, Canadian scholar Eric Valentine Gordon became a lecturer at the University of Leeds alongside Tolkien. The two quickly struck up a friendship, and often collaborated professionally during their time together at Leeds. First, they worked together on a glossary of Middle English terms, titled *A Middle English Vocabulary*. Initially, this glossary was intended to be published with New Zealand publisher Kenneth Sisam's poetry collection, *Fourteenth Century Verse and Prose*. However, the glossary wasn't finished in time for the collection's 1921 publication date. It was instead published separately in 1922, then included in later editions of Sisam's collection. Tolkien and Gordon then went on to translate the Middle English epic poems *Sir Gawain and the Green Knight* (more on this later) and *Pearl*, as well as the Anglo-Saxon poems *The Wanderer* and *The Seafarer*.

THE MORE YOU KNOW

Though translated during their time together at Leeds, *Pearl* and *The Seafarer* weren't published until much later, by Gordon's wife, Ida. *Pearl* was published in 1953 with an introduction by Tolkien, and *The Seafarer* was published in 1960.

The two friends also formed the Viking Club, dedicated to drinking beer, reading Old Icelandic sagas, and singing songs in Old Norse. Most of the songs were written by Tolkien and Gordon themselves, and included cheeky verses about the undergraduate students. This made them rather a popular duo among students and faculty alike at the University of Leeds. There is at least one book containing some of these songs (found at the University of Leeds and called *Songs for the Philologists*). The book was published by other members of the faculty without Tolkien's or Gordon's knowledge. It is now considered a highly sought-after collector's item of immense value in the Tolkien community. Of the many copies printed, most were lost to time or in a fire. Estimates are that only fourteen copies currently survive!

The friendship between Gordon and Tolkien was cut short. Tolkien would take a job at the University of Oxford in 1925, while Gordon stayed at Leeds until 1931 before becoming a professor at the University of Manchester. The two continued to exchange letters until tragedy struck; in 1938, E.V. Gordon passed away due to complications with gallstones. Tolkien mourned the loss, having referred to Gordon as his "devoted friend and pal," and "an industrious little devil."

Sir Gawain and the Green Knight

The most well-known of J.R.R. Tolkien and E.V. Gordon's collaborative works is the translation of *Sir Gawain and the Green Knight*. The idea for its translation first came about when Tolkien first stumbled upon the legend and realized that no edition was available for his university students. So, he and Gordon started working on a more modern edition—Tolkien handling the translation and Gordon the notes.

Sir Gawain and the Green Knight is a fourteenth-century tale about a knight in King Arthur's court. In the tale, a knight with green skin arrives at King Arthur's court during a New Year's Eve feast and challenges any member of the court to battle. Whoever could best the Green Knight would be allowed to strike his attacker with his own axe, on the condition that the Green Knight strike a similar blow a year and a day later. Sir Gawain accepts the challenge and beheads the knight, who then picks up his own head and rides away on his horse. Through a series of adventures, temptations, and deceitful behavior, Gawain finds the Green Knight one year and a day later. He kneels in front of the knight, wearing a green sash he believes will make him invulnerable. But Gawain discovers the Green Knight is someone he met earlier in the story, and the whole quest was meant to test

Arthur's knights. Gawain is dealt only a slight nick to the side of his neck and chastised for his deceitful use of the green sash. Gawain then rejoins the Knights of the Round Table, who all choose to wear a green sash in honor of his adventure and as a reminder to stay honest.

Tolkien and Gordon published their translation of *Sir Gawain and the Green Knight* in 1925.

The More You Know

J.R.R. Tolkien's translation of *Sir Gawain and the Green Knight* was quite popular and went on to receive multiple printings and a variety of different editions eventually edited by his son, Christopher. Later editions feature translations of two other Middle English poems: *Pearl* and *Sir Orfeo*. Later editions also list Tolkien and Gordon as the authors, rather than the translators, of the Sir Gawain story.

From Sir Gawain and the Green Knight

If any so hardy in this house here holds that he is,
if so bold be his blood or his brain be so wild,
that he stoutly dare strike one stroke for another,
then I will give him as my gift this guisarme costly,
this axe—'tis heavy enough—to handle as he pleases;
and I will abide the first brunt, here bare as I sit.
If any fellow be so fierce as my faith to test,
hither let him haste to me and lay hold of this weapon—
I hand it over for ever, he can have it as his own—
and I will stand a stroke from him,
stock-still on this floor,
provided thou'lt lay down this law:
that I may deliver him another.

Professor Tolkien

The Reader position at Leeds proved fruitful for J.R.R. Tolkien, and not just because of his friendship and collaborations with scholar E.V. Gordon. Just four years after accepting the position, he was promoted to the role of professor in 1924. Tolkien continued to lecture and research and also continued to write during this time of his life. Privately he still developed the Elvish language and wrote poetry. He also continued to work on *The Book of Lost Tales*. The interconnected mythos of Middle-earth continued to blossom as stories became intrinsically linked together in Tolkien's imagination.

Just a year after his promotion, the professorship of Anglo-Saxon at Oxford became available in 1925, and Tolkien got the job. "And after this, you might say, nothing else really happened," joked Humphrey Carpenter in his Tolkien biography. By most accounts, Tolkien went on to live an uneventful life, while also writing four of the bestselling books of all time. Now the Rawlinson and Bosworth Professor of Anglo-Saxon, J.R.R. Tolkien was about to be a household name.

The More You Know

J.R.R. Tolkien was a "linguaphile": a language and word lover. This word comes from the Latin root *Lingu*, meaning "tongue," and the suffix *-phile*, which means "lover of."

Tolkien's Anglo-Saxon Fascination

The Anglo-Saxons were a people who inhabited what is now England and parts of Scotland for around six hundred years (around A.D. 410 until A.D. 1066). Known as "farmer-warriors," they were made up of tribes from Germany, Denmark, and the Netherlands. A professorship in Anglo-Saxon language and literature was a fitting role for Tolkien, who loved the Anglo-Saxons, although he tried to avoid the term "Anglo-Saxon," instead preferring "Old English." And with his interest in languages, it is no wonder that Tolkien would continue in his role as a professor of Anglo-Saxon at Pembroke College, Oxford, for twenty years. He considered the Anglo-Saxon language complex, especially considering that, prior to the Latin alphabet being introduced to the British Isles around the sixth century, Anglo-Saxon was written in a runic script (runes are letters of a Germanic alphabet first used around the first century A.D.).

Tolkien's interest in the Anglo-Saxon language and history had a profound impact on his own writing. There are dozens of references to Anglo-Saxon culture found within Middle-earth; the dwarven king Thror's map described in

The Hobbit contains Anglo-Saxon runes. Professor Tolkien also incorporated the Old English language into the fictional language of the people of Rohan (sometimes called Rohirric or Rohanese). The term "Théoden King" is believed to be revived from the title used by Alfred the Great: Alfred Kunish, which translates to "Alfred King."

Even some of the landscape and architecture of Middle-earth derive from Anglo-Saxon culture and literature. The Golden Hall of Meduseld where Théoden King sits and governs Rohan was inspired by the golden mead hall of King Hrothgar in the Old English epic poem *Beowulf*: "the timbered hall, splendid and gold-adorned—the most famous building among men under the heavens—where the high king waited."

Christopher Tolkien would publish some of his father's Old English writings in *The Shaping of Middle-earth* (the fourth volume of The History of Middle-earth), leaving them untranslated.

THE MORE YOU KNOW

While Tolkien drew inspiration from *Beowulf*, his own works have inspired and influenced books, movies, TV shows, and games for decades. J.K. Rowling's Harry Potter series and George R.R. Martin's A Song of Ice and Fire series are influenced by Tolkien, as are the Star Wars movie series and the TV adaptation of A Song of Ice and Fire, *Game of Thrones*.

The Professor and Philology

Philology is the study of languages in both a historical and a comparative context. It is also the true heart of J.R.R. Tolkien's professional career. Working as a researcher for a dictionary and a Reader for a university certainly helped. But it wasn't until Tolkien accepted the job as a professor of Anglo-Saxon language and literature at Oxford in 1925 that his career in the way of words truly started.

Tolkien's love of languages led him to construct his own languages (like the elven languages, explored previously, and the dwarven language, discussed later in this book). It also inspired him to translate works from other writers. Specifically, his fascination with the Anglo-Saxon language led to *Beowulf: A Translation and Commentary*, Tolkien's very own translation of the Old English epic poem. Written by an unknown writer sometime between A.D. 650 and A.D. 800, *Beowulf* follows the titular character on his quest to defeat a troll-creature named Grendel, and then Grendel's vengeful mother. Beowulf is later crowned a king, and before his death, he helps defeat a dragon. The poem is regarded as one of the most important works of Old English and is made up of 3,182 lines. One verse reads, "Thus bemourned the Geatish folk their master's fall, comrades of his hearth, crying that he was ever of the kings of earth of men the most generous and to men most gracious, to his people most tender and for praise most eager."

Considered by many scholars to be one of his most significant contributions to literature, Tolkien started his 425-page translation of *Beowulf* in 1920 and finished it in 1926. However, it didn't see print until much later, when his son Christopher edited and published it posthumously in 2014. (Some believe that Tolkien had been too preoccupied with writing *The Hobbit* to get his translation published in the years after finishing it.) Critics have praised Tolkien's translation for how accurately it follows the details and rhythm of the original version.

LITERARY CONNECTIONS

Before Christopher Tolkien edited and published his father's translation of *Beowulf*, Tolkien scholar Michael D.C. Drout attempted to edit and publish the work. This attempt was canceled by the Tolkien Estate. However, his time with the text led Drout to note that Tolkien's translation remained truer to the original epic poem than any other translation.

Mary Renault

Her legal name was Eileen Mary Challans, but readers knew her as Mary Renault, one of the most well-recognized lesbian authors of LGBTIQA+ fiction of her time. But before she became a popular writer, Mary Renault was a student studying under Professor J.R.R. Tolkien at Oxford.

Renault was born in Oxford in 1905 and started her undergraduate education in 1924 at St. Hugh's College, Oxford, where she was tutored by Tolkien. While at school, she was also encouraged by Tolkien to write a novel set during medieval times. However, she burned the manuscript for the novel, believing it to be inauthentic. After graduating Oxford in 1928 with a degree in English, she started training as a nurse in order to support herself, and it wasn't until 1939 that she published her first novel, *Promise of Love*, under the pseudonym Mary Renault.

Of the fifteen books she published in her lifetime, many take place in Classical Greece and feature gay characters. At the time, homosexuality was illegal in both the UK and the US and was rarely written about in fictional literature. In fact, Renault's book *The Charioteer* (published in London in 1953) was denied publication in the US until 1959, out of fear the publishing company would be prosecuted. *The Charioteer* follows the life and relationships of a gay soldier in World War II. Renault's books became a beacon for the queer community during her lifetime and remain so today.

Tolkien admired Renault's works, writing in one letter that he was "deeply engaged" in her books. He also mentioned that Renault had written "a card of appreciation" to him, which he considered the piece of fan mail that gave him the "most pleasure." Renault and her partner, Julie Mullard, would eventually move to Tolkien's birthplace of South Africa in 1948, where they would spend the rest of their lives. Renault died in 1983, and left instructions for her partner, Julie, to burn her unfinished works and correspondence (which Julie did).

LITERARY CONNECTIONS

Another of the mentees that Tolkien took under his literary wing, Elaine Griffiths, was a chair of the English Faculty Board at St. Anne's College, Oxford. She was an early reader of the manuscript of *The Hobbit* and would later receive a signed copy of The Lord of the Rings—which is part of a private collection at the Greisinger Museum in Switzerland. In Tolkien's inscription, he refers to Elaine as "Queen of Hobbits."

Roverandom

Before there was *The Hobbit,* there was *Roverandom,* a shorter work of children's fantasy. *Roverandom* was J.R.R. Tolkien's attempt to console his younger son, Michael, after the loss of a beloved toy. The toy dog had been lost on a beach while the family was on vacation at the seaside resort of Filey in Yorkshire. *Roverandom* began as a story told to both of Tolkien's sons, John and Michael, during that vacation in 1925, then Tolkien later developed it into a full, written tale.

Roverandom follows an excitable and somewhat ill-mannered dog named Rover. This fictional dog bites a wizard named Artaxerxes, who then refuses to give Rover his ball back and turns Rover into a toy dog. Rover's journey to turn back into a real dog takes him to the moon and under the sea and includes an encounter with a great white dragon. With the help of a sand wizard, Rover is eventually turned back into a real dog.

Tolkien uses his love of all things fairy (more on this later) to weave a tale that is both reassuring and whimsical—and follows the narrative framework he loved so much of combining the ordinary with the extraordinary: "Rover did not know in the least where the moon's path led to, and at present he was much too frightened and excited to ask, and anyway he was beginning to get used to extraordinary things happening to him." As with many of Tolkien's fictional works, the story behind the written story is the heart of the work.

Roverandom also includes hints of Tolkien's love for languages. Several big words found in the story are beyond the grasp of most children in the age range the story was written for (Tolkien's own son Michael was almost five when J.R.R. wrote *Roverandom*). However, that didn't deter Tolkien from using them: Ever the philologist, he believed that a good vocabulary is only learned through reading difficult words, regardless of how old you are!

LITERARY CONNECTIONS

After he wrote *Roverandom,* J.R.R. Tolkien crafted other short works for children, like *Mr. Bliss,* which was first published in book form by Allen & Unwin in 1982. This story, also illustrated by Tolkien, follows the titular character as he takes a ride in a brand-new car. While on this journey, Mr. Bliss has many adventures—which include a run-in with bears! The main plot of the story is based on Tolkien's own troubles with his first car, and the bears in the story were inspired by his sons' toy bears.

From Roverandom

And so at last weeks or months since the tale began (he could not have told you which), he got back to his own garden gate. And there was the little boy playing on the lawn with the yellow ball! And the dream had come true, just as he had never expected!!

"There's Roverandom!!!" cried the little boy Two with a shout.

And Rover sat up and begged, and could not find his voice to back anything, and the little boy kissed his head, and went dashing into the house, crying "here's my little begging dog come back large and real!!!"

Fast Friends

Of the many literary contemporaries J.R.R. Tolkien knew in his life, renowned author C.S. Lewis had one of the greatest impacts on him. The two bonded immediately when they met at a faculty meeting on May 11, 1926. Lewis was then also working as a professor at Oxford (teaching English literature). On top of both being veterans of World War I, Lewis had also lost his mother, Florence (known as Flora), at a young age. He was just nine years old when she passed away from cancer on his father, Albert's, birthday. Then, that same year, Albert Lewis's father and brother also died. C.S. Lewis later reflected on the experience, "With my mother's death, all settled happiness, all that was tranquil and reliable, disappeared from my life. And there had never been really any sense of security and snugness since."

Their childhood experiences of loss, their military service during the Great War, and their mutual interest in writing laid the foundation for a fast friendship. The two would regularly be seen at Oxford drinking at the pub The Eagle and Child with their literary discussion group, the Inklings (more on this group later). Lewis would eventually share his Narnia series with the group, and Tolkien would do the same with most of his writings featuring Middle-earth.

The More You Know

Tolkien's friendship strongly influenced C.S. Lewis to convert to Christianity: "Now what [Hugo] Dyson and Tolkien showed me was this: that if I met the idea of sacrifice in a Pagan story I didn't mind it at all: and again, that if I met the idea of sacrificing himself to himself . . . I liked it very much and was mysteriously moved by it." Lewis later went on to write a paper for the Oxford University Socratic Club in which he acknowledges that he believes in Christianity just as he believes the sun has risen—both because he can see it and because he can see everything else because of it.

By Tolkien's own account, the two men would grow apart in their later years. The time and effort of supporting a family as well as several theological differences led to a cooling of their friendship. Lewis would eventually marry a divorced American named Joy Davidman in 1956, which seemed to drive a wedge between them as well. Tolkien scholar Humphrey Carpenter theorized, "It was almost as if Tolkien felt betrayed by the marriage, resented the intrusion of a woman into his friendship with Lewis." But Tolkien always spoke very highly of Lewis. In a letter to his daughter written just four days after C.S Lewis passed away in 1963, Tolkien wrote: "So far I have felt the normal feelings of a man of my age—like an old tree that is losing all its leaves one by one: this feels like an axe-blow near the roots."

Writing The Hobbit

Though The Lord of the Rings is considered the most popular of Tolkien's fictional works based on the number of copies sold since its publication date, it is nearly impossible to discuss this series without first looking at the children's book that made his publishers ask for a sequel: *The Hobbit.*

Tolkien wrote most of *The Hobbit* while he worked as a professor of Anglo-Saxon at Oxford. According to a letter he wrote to poet W.H. Auden, the inspiration for the book came in 1930 while he was grading exams: "All I remember about the start of The Hobbit is sitting correcting School Certificate papers in the everlasting weariness of that annual task. . . . On a blank leaf I scrawled: 'In a hole in the ground, there lived a hobbit.' I do not know why." This sentence would become the very first line of the final manuscript.

Tolkien continued to write *The Hobbit* over the next two years, taking inspiration from his deep love of the Anglo-Saxon and Norse languages and crafting a tale of adventure—of dragons and hoards of treasure, heroes returning home with a great boon, riddles in the dark places of the world, and a young hero coming of age in a world of wizards and dwarves.

By 1932, the story was nearly complete. Bilbo Baggins had found the magic ring that made him turn invisible. Smaug the dragon had been slain and the dwarves had reclaimed the treasure of Erebor. But *The Hobbit* would sit for nearly five years and go through many revisions before it was finally finished and published by Allen & Unwin in September 1937. Tolkien's son Christopher remarks in one of his commentaries on his father's letters: "This typescript was eventually seen by Susan Dagnall, an Oxford graduate working for the London publishing house Allen & Unwin, and she encouraged Tolkien to complete the story and offer it for publication." Tolkien did just that. Two days after he sent in the completed typescript, Allen & Unwin wrote back that they would give the book their "immediate and careful consideration."

LITERARY CONNECTIONS

The Hobbit is not the first example of the word "hobbit" found in literature. A folklorist named Michael Aislabie Denham published a series of fifty-four pamphlets over thirteen years, from 1846 to 1859, called the Denham Tracts. The word "hobbit" appears on page 79 of the pamphlet titled "Folklore of the North of England." It is unclear if Tolkien knew of this previous instance, though some scholars believe that since Tolkien had a much-publicized love of all things folklore, it is possible he had read the pamphlet. The word "hob" itself is of Middle English origin; it typically means a country fellow, and "Hob" is also a diminutive form of the name Robin.

Norse Mythology

One of J.R.R. Tolkien's influences while writing *The Hobbit*—and all his works set in the fictional Middle-earth—was Norse mythology. Even the land of Middle-earth itself draws parallels to the Norse myth of Midgard, where humans lived.

Tolkien was fascinated by Norse myths. He was particularly interested in the *Saga of the Völsungs,* a thirteenth-century tale based on a collection of anonymous Old Norse poems, the *Elder Edda*. The *Saga of the Völsungs* follows the rise and fall of the Völsung clan. In part of this tale, a cursed hoard of gold is guarded by a dragon; this plot shares similarities with *The Hobbit*'s dragon, Smaug, and the Lonely Mountain where he hoarded riches stolen from dwarves. The dwarves themselves are found within Tolkien's Anglo-Saxon fascination. One portion of the poem *Völuspá,* called *Dvergatal,* also known as The Tally of the Dwarves, contains eight of the thirteen dwarf names found in Thorin's company as well as an early draft of the name Gandalf. The twelve dwarf names are: Nár, Náinn, Nípingr, Dáinn, Bífur, Báfur, Bömbur, Nóri, Órinn, Ónarr, Óinn, Mióðvitnir, Vigr og Gandálfr, Vindálfr, Porinn, Fíli, Kíli, Fundinn, Váli, Þrór, Þróinn, Þettr, Litr, and Vitr.

Additionally, Tolkien's tale of the One Ring in The Lord of the Rings parallels the Norse myth of the Andvaranaut, a cursed ring that leads to much bloodshed and murder. Similar to how Tolkien's One Ring can find the other Rings of Power, the Andvaranaut can find gold.

LITERARY CONNECTIONS

It was J.R.R. Tolkien's love of Norse mythology that led to his co-founding of the Viking Club with E.V. Gordon. The club was meant for philologists and historians (both students and professors) to come together and read Old Icelandic sagas and drink together.

"On Fairy-Stories"

In addition to Norse mythology, Tolkien found inspiration for *The Hobbit* (and his other fantasy works) in stories about fairies. In fact, his fascination with all things fae would lead him to give one of his earliest—and now most famous—lectures, "On Fairy-Stories."

First delivered in 1939 at the University of St. Andrews, Tolkien's "On Fairy-Stories" laid the groundwork for his storytelling technique, and also explored the value of the stories of the fae realm. Many of Tolkien's academic peers had all but dismissed the idea of fantasy literature being taken seriously. But in Tolkien's opinion, fairy stories weren't just meant for children but meant for all. He also believed that fairy stories encompassed any tales or narratives touching on the supernatural or mythical. By his logic, the Norse myths about the likes of Thor and the tales of Camelot's King Arthur (who becomes the king of Faery) are also fairy stories.

It was a defense of the fantastical literature he had grown to love—detailing how the ideas found in mythical tales could be of academic significance. He argued that literary criticism might soon take new form, if only his peers could grasp it.

Literary Connections

It was also in his "On Fairy-Stories" lecture that J.R.R. Tolkien described a key literary term he coined: eucatastrophe. The word combines the Greek prefix *eu*, meaning "good," and the word "catastrophe," meaning "a sudden disaster." A eucatastrophe, explained Tolkien, is a sudden and usually unexpected joyous turn that fills the reader with a sense of hope. A eucatastrophe occurred in *The Hobbit* when Bard the Bowman hit the exact weak spot on the dragon Smaug's body to slay the dragon. In The Lord of The Rings, it happened when Rohan's arrival at Pelennor Fields during the siege at Minas Tirith brought joy to the hearts of Gondorian soldiers.

From "On Fairy-Stories"

For it is man who is, in contrast to fairies, supernatural (and often of diminutive stature); whereas they are natural, far more natural than he. Such is their doom. The road to fairyland is not the road to Heaven; nor even to Hell, I believe, though some have held that it may lead thither indirectly by the Devil's tithe.

Tolkien the Lecturer

Often overshadowed by his popularity as an author, J.R.R. Tolkien was also a professor who needed to make a living. This required him to lecture. As Tolkien scholar Humphrey Carpenter noted, Professor Tolkien was known for being an engaging lecturer, though his style was deemed unconventional at times: "He could laugh at anybody, but most of all at himself, and his complete lack of any sense of dignity could and often did make him behave like a riotous school boy." Though that did not stop him from (seemingly) trying to get away with not doing lectures.

As one of his students, Diana Wynne Jones, recalled: "You couldn't hear him lecture. He worked at not letting you hear, because he wanted to go away and finish writing The Lord of the Rings . . . I imagine I caused Tolkien much grief by turning up to hear him lecture week after week, while he was trying to wrap his lectures up after a fortnight and get on with The Lord of the Rings."

The More You Know

In one example of J.R.R. intentionally making his classes so bad that fewer people would take them and he would have more time to write The Lord of the Rings, he would face the chalkboard for the entire class.

"Beowulf: The Monster and the Critics"

While "On Fairy-Stories" was popular with students at Oxford and provides a glimpse into what inspired Tolkien while he wrote *The Hobbit,* the most well-known of his lectures was on *Beowulf,* the epic poem he had translated back in the 1920s.

"Beowulf: The Monster and the Critics" was given by Tolkien at the British Academy in 1936. *Beowulf* is an Old English epic poem that tells the story of the titular character as he fights a monstrous being known as a Grendel (a supposed descendant of Cain from the Bible), as well as the Grendel's mother. Beowulf eventually becomes king of his people and, in his final act of bravery and heroism, slays a dragon that is ravaging his lands. Before Tolkien's lecture, most scholars had studied *Beowulf* for its significance as a historical text and for its linguistic value. In *his* lecture, Tolkien argued that those scholars missed the point—that *Beowulf* was a good story, and should be examined as such.

Tolkien's lecture acted as a kind of literary criticism on literary criticism. He stated: "It has been said of *Beowulf* itself that its weakness lies in placing the unimportant things at the centre and the important on the outer edge. . . . I think it profoundly untrue of the poem, but strikingly true of the literature about it. . . . Beowulf is in fact so interesting as poetry, in places poetry so powerful, that this quite overshadows the historical content."

THE MORE YOU KNOW

Tolkien is often referred to by the nickname "The Professor" by fans of his work. Every year, on January 3 (Tolkien's birthday), The Tolkien Society welcomes his fans to celebrate with a 9 p.m. toast: To join the celebration, one simply must raise a glass of their favorite libation and exclaim, "The Professor!" before drinking from their glass.

Tolkien the Time Traveler

Walk into most bookstores and you will see the science fiction books next to or combined with the fantasy books. As it happens, J.R.R. Tolkien almost occupied both genres during his time as a professor and master lecturer—thanks to his friendship with C.S. Lewis.

In a letter to writers Charlotte and Denis Plimmer, Tolkien recounted the moment when Lewis said they should try writing science fiction: "L. said to me one day: 'Tollers, there is too little of what we really like in stories. I am afraid we shall have to try and write some ourselves.'" It was decided that Tolkien would focus on time travel in his stories and Lewis on space travel.

Told from the perspective of a father and son through various points in time, the story Tolkien started writing, called "The Lost Road," explores the realm of Númenor: a kind of Atlantis-inspired island between Middle-earth and the Undying Lands (more on this later!). The story would never be completed, however, and Tolkien's publishers, Allen & Unwin, said it likely would not have been a commercial success even if Tolkien *had* finished it. Christopher Tolkien himself called the story "very rough" and lacking "a continuous text."

Tolkien admitted to the Plimmers that he gave up after writing just a few chapters (a similar thing would happen when he attempted to write a sequel to The Lord of the Rings, but more on that later). Tolkien's true focus was on his own version of the myth of Atlantis: "My effort, after a few promising chapters, ran dry: it was too long a way round to what I really wanted to make, a new version of the Atlantis legend."

C.S. Lewis's attempt would be met with more success. He went on to publish The Space Trilogy from 1938 until 1945. The main character of the trilogy is Dr. Elwin Ransom, who is reminiscent of Tolkien. Like Tolkien, Ransom fought in World War I at the Battle of the Somme and was a philologist at Oxford University. Tolkien himself noted the similarities between himself and Lewis's fictional Dr. Ransom: "[A]s a philologist I may have some part in him, and recognize some of my opinions and ideas Lewisified in him."

THE MORE YOU KNOW

While J.R.R. Tolkien abandoned his science fiction quest during his lifetime, readers can thank Christopher Tolkien for bringing it back to life after his father's passing. Tolkien's tale of time travel, while incomplete, is included in the fifth book of his son's The History of Middle-earth series. It consists of four chapters—two of which take place in Númenor.

The Inklings

At the same time that J.R.R. Tolkien and C.S. Lewis were challenging each other to write science fiction, they were also taking part in an exclusive club of Oxford legend called the Inklings. An informal group, the Inklings would meet every Thursday evening to discuss literature. While originally created by undergraduate student Edward Lean at University College, Oxford, the meeting had mostly died out when Lean graduated. From the early 1930s until around 1949, Tolkien and Lewis carried on the club's legacy with people Tolkien later described as "the undetermined and unelected circle of friends who gathered about C.S.L." in a letter to writer William Luther White. Tolkien later went on to note in the letter that the members' habit of reading aloud would have happened naturally, with or without the club, as hearing things read aloud was a passion of C.S. Lewis.

While Tolkien and Lewis were members, the Inklings often congregated in Lewis's rooms at Magdalen College or at the now-famous pub The Eagle and Child. Their discussions primarily related to the members' unfinished works, with Tolkien's Lord of the Rings and Lewis's novel *Out of the Silent Planet* among the first to be discussed by the club.

Other members included Lewis's brother, Warren; Charles Williams; Owen Barfield; and Hugo Dyson.

LITERARY CONNECTIONS

It was fairly common at the time of the Inklings for university literary groups to be exclusively male. However, crime novelist and friend of C.S. Lewis, Dorothy L. Sayers, was sometimes called an Inkling. As she was not a formal member of the club, Dorothy never attended any of the meetings at The Eagle and Child. Sayers is known for her character Lord Peter Wimsey, an amateur detective featured in eleven novels and a number of shorter works.

Tolkien even tried his hand at putting the Inklings on the page. Though he didn't get very far. At the same time as writing *The Lord of the Rings*, Tolkien was also writing a time travel story called "The Notion Club Papers." Presented as a series of fictional documents found after a storm hits Oxford, these diary entries, meeting notes, and letters written by the "Notion Club" were Tolkien's attempt to bring his real-life meetings into the written world. Though never finished and not even published in his lifetime, this attempt at science fiction by The Professor would be made public much later in life thanks to Tolkien's son, Christopher.

Tom Bombadil

Tom Bombadil is considered one of the most interesting yet least characterized enigmas of Tolkien's Middle-earth. Living in the Old Forest, he rescues Frodo, Sam, Merry, and Pippin from the evil Old Man Willow and later from barrow-wights in *The Fellowship of the Ring*. While the hobbits stay at Tom's home in the forest, the One Ring is shown to have no effect on him. When Frodo wears the ring, Tom is still able to see him. Similarly, when Tom puts the ring on his own finger, he stays visible.

Some in the Tolkien community claim that Tom Bombadil is integral to the plot of The Lord of the Rings, while others insist he is an unnecessary addition to the story that distracts from a compelling narrative. In her essay "Who Is Tom Bombadil?" scholar Jane Beal asserts that "he must be interpreted at multiple levels of meaning simultaneously"—as a god-like figure, the embodiment of nature, Adam from the Bible, and Tolkien himself. Whether Tom Bombadil is important to The Lord of the Rings or not, this wasn't the first time Tolkien wrote about the character. He first appeared in a poem titled "The Adventures of Tom Bombadil." Published in 1934 in *The Oxford Magazine*, the poem was written ahead of *The Hobbit*'s publication and describes Tom as a "merry fellow" who defeats evil enchantments with his voice and eventually marries a beautiful woman named Goldberry.

LITERARY CONNECTIONS

Before he made his appearance on the page, Tom Bombadil appeared in real life as a Dutch doll owned by J.R.R.'s son Michael. The doll had hinged joints and was constructed from wooden pegs. Young John Tolkien once threw the doll in the toilet, and after its rescue, J.R.R. went on to tell the first tale of the toy in "The Adventures of Tom Bombadil."

It would be twenty years after "The Adventures of Tom Bombadil" was first published that Tom showed up again, in *The Fellowship of the Ring*, followed by a mention in *The Return of the King*. Bombadil also makes an appearance in a second poem, "Bombadil Goes Boating," which was published by Tolkien alongside the first in 1962 in a poetry collection titled *The Adventures of Tom Bombadil*.

From "The Adventures of Tom Bombadil"

Old Tom Bombadil was a merry fellow;
bright blue his jacket was and his boots were yellow,
green were his girdle and his breeches all of leather;
he wore in his tall hat a swan-wing feather.
He lived up under Hill, where the Withywindle
ran from a grassy well down into the dingle . . .

Dwarven Language

The dwarven language of Middle-earth is known as Khuzdûl. Unlike its Elvish counterpart Sindarin, which is spoken across Middle-earth, Khuzdûl is a closely guarded language spoken only by the dwarves themselves. First appearing in *The Hobbit,* Dwarvish was constructed by Tolkien prior to the book's 1936 publication. It combines the use of three different real languages: Hebrew for many of the root-based word structures, Aramaic for many of the phonetics, and Arabic for the more guttural sounds such as consonants produced toward the back of the vocal tract.

The language itself is mostly a harsh-sounding or guttural language, with many consonants like g, z, k, h, and b clustered together. The word the dwarves of Middle-earth have for themselves is Khazâd. The ancient and abandoned city explored by The Fellowship on their quest to destroy the ring is called Khazad-dûm. In writing the language, the dwarves use the runic script typically used in stone carving, known as Cirth, which means "runes" in Sindarin. A full list of each of the Cirth runes can be found in The Appendices of *The Return of the King.*

Tolkien's dwarves prefer to keep to themselves and show a strong prejudice toward the other races in Middle-earth.

The Khuzdûl language plays a part in keeping them closed off from the world, as Tolkien noted in a letter to the editor of *The Observer* newspaper: "Dwarvish was both complicated and cacophonous. Even early Elvish philologists avoided it, and the dwarves were obliged to use other languages, except for in entirely private conversations." Given this penchant for keeping their language hidden, the dwarves choose to learn other languages instead of teaching Khuzdûl to others.

THE MORE YOU KNOW

The private nature of the dwarves in Middle-earth extend to their names: Their given names are kept secret from outsiders. Because of this, their names are not even inscribed on their tombs, in case a stranger would happen upon the tomb and read the inscription.

The Tale of Rayner Unwin

J.R.R. Tolkien knew that those of a smaller stature could accomplish the great deeds of the world: "Yet such is oft the course of deeds that move the wheels of the world: small hands do them because they must, while the eyes of the great are elsewhere," says Elrond in *The Fellowship of the Ring*. And it pleased him to no end when a ten-year-old named Rayner Unwin convinced his father, Sir Stanley Unwin, to publish *The Hobbit*.

Sir Stanley Unwin was one of the two founders of the publishing firm Allen & Unwin, the company that would ultimately publish *The Hobbit*, as well as The Lord of the Rings trilogy. When he was a young boy, Unwin's son, Rayner, worked as a test reader for Allen & Unwin; Sir Stanley credited children as the best judges for what qualified as a good children's book and would pay 1 shilling for every report Rayner wrote about a book the company was considering publishing.

On October 30, 1936, Rayner wrote a book report of *The Hobbit* (believed to be the first review of the book). Sir Unwin paid his son the typical shilling for the review, which Rayner later noted turned out to be "the best shilling our firm ever spent." After providing a summary of *The Hobbit*,

Rayner Unwin's report went on to describe the book as suitable for young children. He would later say that while this early review may not have been the best piece of literary criticism, it still led to *The Hobbit*'s publication by Allen & Unwin in September of the following year.

THE MORE YOU KNOW

***The Hobbit* was not Rayner's only major credit to children's literature. When he began working for Allen & Unwin in adulthood, he was entranced by a copy of *James and the Giant Peach* that Tessa Dahl (Roald Dahl's daughter), a schoolfriend of Rayner's daughter Camilla, had given Camilla. Rayner was responsible for the first UK publications of Roald Dahl's *James and the Giant Peach* (1961) and *Charlie and the Chocolate Factory* (1964).**

Without Raynor's insight as a child himself, many believe the epic tales of Bilbo Baggins may not have been brought into the spotlight. Rayner's keen eye for a good story also led to a successful career as an editor for his father's company. Developing a close friendship with Tolkien, Rayner would eventually work with him on The Lord of the Rings series beginning in 1952, more than fifteen years after his childhood report on *The Hobbit.*

From Rayner Unwin's Report on The Hobbit

Bilbo Baggins was a Hobbit who lived in his Hobbit hole and never went for adventures, at last Gandalf the wizard and his Dwarves persuaded him to go. He had a very exciting (sic) time fighting goblins and wargs. At last they get to the lonely mountain; Smaug, the dragon who guards it is killed and after a terrific battle with the goblins he returned home—rich!
This book, with the help of maps, does not need any illustrations. It is good and should appeal to all children between the ages of 5 and 9.

A Certain Point of View

J.R.R. Tolkien never meant for *The Hobbit* to be included as part of the larger mythos of *The Silmarillion*. But that's not for lack of trying once The Lord of the Rings gained popularity. Readers will find a chapter in *Unfinished Tales of Númenor and Middle-earth* (published much later, in 1980) that provides a slightly different recounting of *The Hobbit*. Written from Frodo's perspective but with most of the story told through Gandalf's narration, this chapter is titled "The Quest of Erebor."

In the tale, Gandalf explains to Frodo why he took it upon himself to recruit Thorin and his company of dwarves, as well as Bilbo, to retake the Lonely Mountain: "You may think that Rivendell was out of his reach, but I did not think so. The state of things in the North was very bad. . . . Often I said to myself: 'I must find some means of dealing with Smaug. But a direct stroke against Dol Guldur is needed still more. We must disturb Sauron's plan.'" Knowing that Sauron would be significantly more powerful with a dragon like Smaug on his side, Gandalf sought to draw out and defeat the dragon before the two villains could join forces.

This different perspective of the tale of *The Hobbit* also paints the characters in a slightly different light. In this version, Thorin is much more severe. When Gandalf says about a map: "Well your father gave me this map ninety-one years ago. And I have guarded it ever since." Thorin replies, "For ninety-one years you have kept my property?" Thorin is also much less trusting of Bilbo and questions his ability to help the dwarves defeat Smaug. Character changes like this were common throughout Tolkien's writing process. Tolkien was driven to construct first the world that characters would live and act in, and only then the characters to inhabit the world, leading to a lot of revisions.

The More You Know

Bilbo was chosen by Gandalf for the quest to defeat Smaug for many reasons—primarily, the dragon would not be familiar with a hobbit's scent, which would ensure stealth on this mission. Bilbo, a much more curious and adventurous sort than the typical hobbit, was generally interested in the world outside the Shire, which led to Gandalf's belief that he would be a fitting companion on the quest. While Thorin was against Bilbo's aid, Gandalf was able to convince him that Bilbo had much to offer.

Smaug and Other Dragons

Whether breathing their scorching fire over the armies of elves, dwarves, and men in the First Age, or resting on their hoards of treasure in The Third Age, dragons were fascinating to J.R.R. Tolkien. He borrowed from different mythologies to create Middle-earth dragons—or "Great Worms," as he sometimes referred to them. As he once said, "I desired dragons with a profound desire. Of course I in my timid body did not wish to have them in the neighborhood."

Tolkien's influences for Smaug, the primary antagonist of *The Hobbit*, were from *Beowulf* and other Norse myths—particularly the dragon Fáfnir from the Saga of the Völsungs. In this myth, Fáfnir is actually a man who gets turned into a dragon due to his greed. Smaug takes after Fáfnir's desire for treasure and is greedy for the dwarven wealth of the Lonely Mountain.

THE MORE YOU KNOW

The word "dragon" is derived from the Greek word *drakōn*, meaning "serpent."

Contrary to Tolkien's tales, many Eastern cultures associate dragons with luck and good fortune. For example, the dragon of the Chinese zodiac is considered to be a particularly lucky sign. Tolkien's dragons were anything but.

For Tolkien, a dragon was something to be feared, not befriended. Their power wreaked havoc on the battlefields of Middle-earth and left many great kingdoms in ruin. Look no further than the destructive nature of dragons in Tolkien's legendarium. His mightiest dragon, Ancalagon the Black, was first described in an early draft of *The Silmarillion* in the 1930s as a creature so huge that when he fell, he shattered the mountain peaks of Thangorodrim (three volcanic mountains serving as furnaces for the smithies of the evil Morgoth's fortress, Angband).

Tolkien believed that dragons could also bring about the destruction of the mind, in addition to physically destroying worlds. In an early draft of *The Children of Húrin* (more on this later), Glaurung of the First Age (sometimes called the Father of Dragons) sets a trap for the hero Túrin Turambar, tricking Túrin's own sister into falling in love with Túrin. And in *The Hobbit,* Smaug has the ability to bring about dragon-sickness, a curse in which the gold a dragon had hoarded causes the new owner to go mad obsessing over it.

Having been mostly killed off during the War of Wrath in the First Age of Middle-earth, dragons would be mentioned only briefly in Tolkien's Lord of the Rings trilogy. For the most part, just the legends of ancient ice drakes in the northernmost parts of Middle-earth continued on after the First Age.

Writing The Lord of the Rings

How exactly did the Father of Modern Fantasy write the three books that got him this title? It took quite a long time—twelve years in fact! (Although much of the groundwork for these books started in the 1910s when Tolkien created his Elvish languages and began creating Middle-earth.) He first started writing the trilogy after the initial success of *The Hobbit* in 1937. *The Hobbit* was so well-received by audiences that his publishers wanted a sequel.

In December 1937, Tolkien crafted a new protagonist for this sequel, Bingo Baggins, who would later be renamed Frodo. In his initial draft, Tolkien had Frodo come into possession of a ring that was just a simple magical object with nothing evil about it. But the story soon turned more sinister as The Professor kept writing. In a letter to his publishers in March 1938, he wrote, "The sequel to *The Hobbit* has now progressed as far as the end of the third chapter. But stories tend to get out of hand, and this has taken an unpremeditated turn. Mr. Lewis [C.S. Lewis] and my youngest boy [Christopher] are reading it in bits as a serial."

Writing was slow and sporadic over the next decade, with numerous distractions coming at Tolkien from all sides. Family life, work duties at Oxford, and of course World War

II all impacted the writing process. “I have worked under difficulties of all kinds, including ill-health. Since the beginning of December I have not been able to touch it,” Tolkien wrote to his editors in 1939. “I then caught influenza, from which I have just recovered. But I have other heavy tasks ahead. I am at the ‘peak’ of my educational financial stress, with a second son clamouring for a university and the youngest wanting to go to school.” Tolkien also had his doubts readers would even like the sequel, despite considering it a much better work himself.

LITERARY CONNECTIONS

When it finally came time to print Tolkien’s monumental work, well, that was another matter entirely. The final manuscript was over 1,200 pages, but that is the revised material. Original versions of Tolkien’s manuscript were well over nine thousand pages long!

A "Small" Inquiry Gone Awry

While J.R.R. Tolkien was writing his sequel to *The Hobbit,* a second World War was beginning. Officially starting in September 1939 when Germany invaded Poland and lasting until Japan's surrender in September 1945, World War II is still considered the deadliest war in history. It was also the second world war that Tolkien would experience in his lifetime. Regarding his experience with two major wars, he said, "I have in this War a burning private grudge—which would probably make me a better soldier at 49 than I was at 22; against that ruddy little ignoramus Adolf Hitler."

Tolkien wasn't a fan of his works being compared to the war, once saying he "cordially dislike[d] allegory in all its manifestations." Yet that did not stop readers both then and now from drawing comparisons between works like *The Hobbit* and The Lord of the Rings and World War II. The Second World War also affected Tolkien's writing career when his publishers, Allen & Unwin, were negotiating with German publishing agency Rütten & Loening in 1938 to print a German translation of *The Hobbit.* Things went awry when Rütten & Loening asked for proof that the author was *arisch* (Aryan). Tolkien was furious. "[D]o their lunatic laws require a certificate of 'arisch' origin from all persons of all countries?" he wrote to his publishers. "[L]et a German translation go hang. . . . I have many Jewish friends, and should regret giving any colour to the notion that I subscribe to the wholly pernicious and unscientific race-doctrine."

Tolkien sent two different responses to his publishers—one that completely ignored the request for proof of his ancestry, and one that included this note: "But if I am to understand that you are enquiring whether I am of *Jewish* origin, I can only reply that I regret that I appear to have *no* ancestors of that gifted people." It's believed that his publishers sent this second response to the German publishers.

LITERARY CONNECTIONS

In the 2008 book *British Children's Fiction in the Second World War*, it is noted that the friendship between Gimli and Legolas, who move past the mutual suspicion that dwarves and elves typically have of each other, can be thought of as Tolkien's rebuff to the anti-Semitism that World War II brought to the forefront at that time.

The War of the Machines

Tolkien's profound love of the natural world became the fulcrum for much of his life's work, including The Lord of the Rings. His childhood was spent among the hills, lakes, and forests of England, and his young adult life started with the destruction of a sizable portion of Europe. He grew up in an age where long-range artillery could level an entire forest in a few hours. He also spent much of his later years watching industrialization overwhelm the once green parts of England.

Trees in particular held a kind of special symbolism in Tolkien's works. The White Tree of Gondor is a place of reverence in the city of Minas Tirith; Galadriel's gift to Samwise in the elven kingdom of Lothlórien is the seed of a tree from her forest; and the source of all light in the Undying Lands was, at one point, the light of two trees, Laurelin and Telperion, known as the Two Trees of Valinor. Throughout Tolkien's writings, trees are a source of comfort and healing—but also a means of defeating industrialization. Just look at Treebeard and his Ents as they march from Fangorn Forest to Isengard to destroy the machines made by the traitorous wizard Saruman. (More later on the Ents and their victory over machines!)

Tolkien also had a love for the water that gave life to the trees. It was water that destroyed the machines of Isengard in *The Two Towers*. The elves awakened into consciousness by Lake Cuiviénen under the stars in the time before even the First Age of Middle-earth. Elves would continue to feel a pull toward the sea in Middle-earth, and would often sail "into the West" to the Undying Lands.

THE MORE YOU KNOW

In a letter to his son Christopher in 1945 expressing his thoughts on World War II, Tolkien grieved that there was no compassion left in the world and that the first "War of the Machines" was pointing to the machines as the victors: "The appalling destruction and misery of this war mount hourly. . . . [T]he first War of the Machines seems to be drawing to its final inconclusive chapter—leaving, alas, everyone the poorer, many bereaved or maimed and millions dead, and only one thing triumphant: the Machines."

"Except Shakespeare (Which I Dislike Cordially)"

J.R.R. Tolkien's portrayals of nature and its triumph over machines in The Lord of the Rings were also influenced by another great writer: William Shakespeare. However, in Tolkien's case, it was a dislike of the Bard's work that helped shaped his story. Two of the most successful literary figures of the last six hundred years, Tolkien and Shakespeare did not seen eye to eye about how forests and fairytale creatures should be handled in their stories.

In Shakespeare's play *Macbeth*, the titular character has no fear of defeat. Three witches had told him that he would never be vanquished "until the Great Birnam Wood to high Dunsinane hill shall come against him." Macbeth is convinced he is unstoppable since trees can't "come against him"; in the end, Macbeth's defeat comes at the hands of British soldiers who disguise themselves with the branches of Birnam Wood.

When the school-age Tolkien read this play, he didn't like it. He later recounted in a letter to W.H. Auden his "bitter disappointment and disgust from schooldays of the shabby use made in Shakespeare [in *Macbeth*] of the coming of 'Great Birnam wood to high Dunsinane hill.'" He was shocked that the Bard would default to a technicality, and this "bitter disappointment" would lead to one of Tolkien's most iconic moments in The Lord of the Rings trilogy: He deploys sentient trees, known as the Ents of Fangorn Forest, a foil to the poorly disguised British soldiers in *Macbeth*. In Tolkien's case, the trees really do take up arms (and occasionally large boulders) against the fortress of Isengard. Using their enormous strength, the Ents win the day by flooding Isengard, destroying the dam that blocked a nearby river. Tolkien satisfied his mission of having "longed to devise a setting in which the trees might really march to war."

It should be noted that Tolkien did not hate Shakespeare's plays; rather, he disliked reading them and instead preferred to see them performed. He even mentions in one letter, "But it emphasized more strongly than anything I have ever seen the folly of reading Shakespeare . . . , except as a concomitant of seeing his plays acted."

Literary Connections

Tree spirits that mimic Tolkien's sentient trees appear in his friend C.S. Lewis's Chronicles of Narnia. And Treebeard himself, the leader of the Ents in Tolkien's series, was based on Lewis (specifically his booming oratorial voice and commanding presence).

Closing Lines of "Song of the Ent and Entwife"

Ent:

When Winter comes, the winter wild that hill and
  wood shall slay;
When trees shall fall and starless night devour
  the sunless day;
When wind is in the deadly East, then in the bitter rain
I'll look for thee, and call to thee;
  I'll come to thee again!

Entwife:

When Winter comes, and singing ends;
  when darkness falls at last;
When broken is the barren bough, and light and
  labour past;
I'll look for thee, and wait for thee, until we
  meet again:
Together we will take the road beneath the bitter rain!

Both:

Together we will take the road that leads into the West,
And far away will find a land where both our
  hearts may rest.

"Wheelbarrows at 5 a.m."

Invitations to parties rarely get mentioned in the footnotes of history. Yet Professor and Mrs. Tolkien requested the pleasure of guests' company on a November evening in 1945 in such a memorable way that it is still discussed today! Published in a tribute to J.R.R.'s youngest son, *The Great Tales Never End: Essays in Memory of Christopher Tolkien*, the invitation in question was to a coming-of-age party for Christopher. The young Tolkien had spent the last two years in the Royal Air Force in South Africa, where he was stationed in Kroonstad (roughly 130 miles from his father's childhood home, Bloemfontein).

His return to England in 1945 was a momentous occasion not just for his safe return and a celebration of his birthday: Christopher Tolkien had also been informed by his father that the Inklings wished to induct him as a member of their club—permanently. Then twenty-one years old, Christopher was the youngest member of the renowned group. He had spent the better part of his life growing up listening to his father's stories and had on occasion been at those meetups at The Eagle and Child pub. (When Christopher passed away in January 2020, Tolkien fans across the globe mourned the loss of "The Last Inkling.")

The details of the party are not known to the public, but fans and Tolkien scholars continue to speculate about the possibilities for entertainment given J.R.R.'s penchant for mischief and pranks. The invitation implied that a rather fascinating ride home awaited the guests: "Carriages at midnight. Ambulances at 2 a.m. Wheelbarrows at 5 a.m. Hearses at daybreak." The party was scheduled to start at 6:30 in the evening, and the Tolkiens specified no end time for the festivities. Instead, the invitation simply said "onwards." The invitation also included a cheeky note to RSVP only if the guest wasn't coming.

THE MORE YOU KNOW

In 1946, the year after his formal invitation to the Inklings, Christopher Tolkien resumed his studies at Trinity College, Oxford, where he was tutored by Oxford professor and his father's dear friend, C.S. Lewis. Much like his father, Christopher showed an interest in Old and Middle English, which he eventually went on to teach at Oxford.

"Leaf by Niggle"

Despite his insistence that his stories in Middle-earth were not allegorical in any way, J.R.R. Tolkien is known by scholars and fans alike for being good at writing allegory. The Professor's non-Middle-earth-related literature showcasing his talents include his short story "Leaf by Niggle."

The story was originally published in *The Dublin Review* in early 1945, the same year the Tolkiens threw their legendary party for Christopher. Of the writing process for this work, Tolkien said, "I woke up one morning . . . with that odd thing virtually complete in my head. It only took a few hours to get down, and then copy out." "Leaf by Niggle" tells the tale of a very busy artist named Niggle attempting to finish a painting of a tree. But at the same time, he is also preparing for a mysterious journey. Niggle finds himself unable to finish his painting or his preparations for the trip because he is beset on all sides by menial tasks.

After falling ill, Niggle is unjustly taken away by the authorities to do even more menial tasks at an institution. He does so until he is taken to a forest where he finds that his unfinished painting of a tree has become a real and living tree. Eventually, he ventures farther into the woods and beyond, to far-off mountains. The narrator mentions that Niggle's old house has been repossessed, and his name and artistic works are all but forgotten. The only remaining evidence of Niggle's artwork is a scrap of the painting of the tree. The scrap of art contains only a single leaf.

"Leaf by Niggle" is often interpreted as an allegory for Tolkien's own creative process, as well as an attempt to explain his concept of "sub-creation." Sub-creation is the idea that true creation is only done by God, and all other creations are just echoes or mockeries of true creation. As Tolkien said himself, sub-creation is "that liberation 'from the channels the creator is known to have used already' . . . a tribute to the infinity of His potential variety."

This somewhat autobiographical allegory finds Tolkien longing to not be bothered with the everyday, mundane tasks so often required of him. In addition to featuring the idea of sub-creation, the story also serves as a kind of allegory for Tolkien's religious beliefs regarding the cycle from life, to death, to purgatory, and, finally, to heaven.

LITERARY CONNECTIONS

The character of Niggle is often compared to that of Dante in Dante Alighieri's *Divine Comedy*. Written more than six hundred years before Tolkien's own allegory, Dante's epic poem describes one man's journey through the three realms of the afterlife: Inferno (Hell), Purgatorio (Purgatory), and Paradiso (Heaven).

Farmer Giles of Ham

The latter half of the 1940s saw Tolkien's life shift academically. In 1945, he would switch jobs at Oxford. No longer the Rawlinson and Bosworth Chair of Anglo-Saxon (a position he held for twenty years), Tolkien was now the Merton Professor of English Language and Literature. He continued to work on his mythos, writing the first drafts of many of the most famous chapters of The Lord of the Rings at this time. But another story was about to come into his mind.

Published in 1949, *Farmer Giles of Ham* is the tale of a simple farmer with the unusually long name of Ægidius Ahenobarbus Julius Agricola de Hammo. But most people just call him Farmer Giles. The story itself is a whimsical and farcical take on dragon-slaying tales. Farmer Giles lives in the Middle Kingdom, a medieval fantasyland filled with giants and dragons. One day while Farmer Giles is out in his fields, a giant stumbles onto his property. Farmer Giles uses a blunderbuss (a short-barreled, muzzle-loading firearm) to scare away the giant and is hailed as a hero of the countryside. The king of this medieval land takes notice of Giles, gives him a sword, and asks him to slay a dragon named Chrysophylax Dives. Farmer Giles is able to subdue the dragon, and eventually becomes the ruler of the land.

The story emphasizes the importance of the courage and bravery of everyday people, and Farmer Giles is often compared by readers to Tolkien's later hero, Samwise Gamgee.

LITERARY CONNECTIONS

Pauline Baynes, the woman who illustrated all seven books of C.S. Lewis's Chronicles of Narnia, was also the illustrator for *Farmer Giles of Ham*. This was not Baynes's only assignment illustrating Tolkien's works: She also illustrated *The Adventures of Tom Bombadil* and *Smith of Wootton Major*, and her cover illustrations for both *The Hobbit* and the single-volume edition of The Lord of the Rings are well-known.

From Father Giles of Ham

That was quite enough for Tailbiter. It circled flashing in the air; then down it came, smiting the dragon on the joint of the right wing, a ringing blow that shocked him exceedingly. Of course Giles knew very little about the methods of killing a dragon, or the sword might have landed in a tenderer spot; but Tailbiter did the best it could in inexperienced hands. It was quite enough for Chrysophylax—he could not use his wing for days.

The Second Version of *The Hobbit*

While he was busily writing The Lord of the Rings, Professor J.R.R. Tolkien was also revising *The Hobbit* so the story of Bilbo would better align with the story of Frodo and the other eight members of the Fellowship of the Ring.

One of the most noticeable changes involves the One Ring itself. In the first edition of *The Hobbit,* published in 1937, Gollum is perfectly fine in betting his magic ring during a game of riddles with Bilbo. He even offers to show Bilbo the way out of his cave. But in order for the ring to play a more central role in the legendarium of Middle-earth, that magic ring was changed in *The Hobbit* to the One Ring forged by Sauron in the fires of Mount Doom. Readers of the second edition of *The Hobbit* find a much angrier Gollum, who does not lead Bilbo out of the cave and who wants the ring back.

Known to be a perfectionist, Tolkien even decided to make an in-universe reason for the changes between the first and second editions of *The Hobbit.* In the chapter of *The Fellowship of the Ring* called "The Council of Elrond," Bilbo admits to the lie he told about his encounter with Gollum: "'Very well,' said Bilbo. 'I will do as you bid. But I will now tell the true story, and if some here have heard otherwise'—he looked sidelong at Glóin—'I ask them to forget it and forgive me. I only wished to claim the treasure as my very own in those days, and be rid of the name of thief that was put on me. But perhaps I understand things a little better now.'"

Another change from the first edition is the removal of the word "gnomes," which originally described the Noldor, also known as the Deep Elves. As "gnome" was thought by Tolkien to stem from the Greek word meaning "knowledge," it originally seemed fitting to describe the wisest of the elves. However, the definition of the word in English—that of a kind of misshapen dwarf—led to Tolkien removing it from subsequent editions.

LITERARY CONNECTIONS

Gollum, whose name was Sméagol before being corrupted by the One Ring, draws a parallel to Cain from the Bible. Both are tragic figures who commit murder against a close relative out of jealousy: Cain against his brother, and Sméagol against his cousin Déagol after the latter hobbit finds a "beautiful golden ring" and refuses to give it to Sméagol. For both Cain and Sméagol, these acts lead to a life of isolation.

From Tolkien's Letter to Allen & Unwin, August 1, 1950

I must say that I could wish that I had had some hint that (in any circumstances) this change might be made, before it burst on me in page-proofs. However, I have now made up my mind to accept the change and its consequences. . . . [I]t seems to me the revised version is in itself better, in motive and narrative—and certainly would make the sequel (if ever published) much more natural.

Publishing Roadblocks

Once finished, J.R.R. Tolkien's Lord of the Rings manuscript was a total of 9,250 pages long! Tolkien wanted to print the manuscript as one book at first, then perhaps two. His publishers, meanwhile, insisted on making it a trilogy. However, Tolkien didn't think the word "trilogy" accurately described this story of the Third Age of Middle-earth. He told Unwin's son, Rayner: "The (unavoidable) disadvantage of issuing in three pans has been shown in the 'shapelessness' that several readers have found, since that is true if one volume is supposed to stand alone. 'Trilogy', which is not really accurate, is partly to blame. There is too much 'hobbitry' in Vol. I taken by itself; and several critics have obviously not got far beyond Chapter I."

The shortage of paper as a consequence of World War II made publishing Tolkien's manuscript as one book financially unfeasible at the time. The recordkeeping required of the massive military forces at work around the world had demanded massive amounts of paper. To outweigh the publishing company's cost to produce the entire Lord of the Rings trilogy in one book, readers would have had to pay 3 pounds 10 sterling (adjusted for inflation, that's around $92 in US dollars today) to purchase a copy. As Sir Stanley Unwin wrote in 1950, replying to one of Tolkien's letters: "It would not have been easy to solve before the War; it is much more difficult now, with costs of production about three times what they were then."

The More You Know

Marquette University purchased the original manuscript of The Lord of the Rings trilogy for a little less than $5,000 (£1,500) in 1956. This purchase also included working drafts of *The Hobbit* and *Farmer Giles of Ham*.

To make matters even more challenging, Tolkien also wanted to publish his stories from *The Silmarillion* alongside The Lord of the Rings, creating a kind of duology that contained the entire narrative of the First, Second, and Third Ages of Middle-earth. Unwin was against this, believing that *The Silmarillion* would not sell, as test readers were much less enthusiastic about this work. So, for the time being at least, *The Silmarillion* remained unpublished.

The publishers and Tolkien would eventually decide to split The Lord of the Rings story into three volumes.

Publishing The Lord of the Rings

Tolkien almost gave the publishing rights to the London publisher Collins when he was introduced to an editor there, Milton Waldman, in 1949. Tolkien hoped Collins would publish The Lord of the Rings as well as *The Silmarillion.* (Something Allen & Unwin had said was likely not feasible.) But Collins also hesitated. By the spring of 1952, Tolkien told them to publish The Lord of the Rings immediately or he would withdraw the manuscript. Collins declined.

Ultimately, the six "books" of The Lord of The Rings were published in three volumes, two "books" per volume by Allen & Unwin. The first two volumes were published in 1954: *The Fellowship of the Ring* on July 29, and *The Two Towers* on November 11. The plan was to publish all three volumes on the same date, but, as with many aspects of Tolkien's writing, he wanted more, and insisted on adding appendices to the third volume before its publication. It was a slow process for The Professor, and he became rather frustrated with it: "I regret that I have not yet any copy to send in for the Appendices. All I can say is that I will do my best to produce this before the end of the month." Finally, the appendices were finished, and the third volume was published on October 20, 1955. Each volume was priced at 21 shillings.

Reviews were mixed at the time of the trilogy's release. Writer Naomi Mitchison called it "a great imaginative achievement" and author (and friend of Tolkien) C.S. Lewis called it a "heroic romance, gorgeous, eloquent, and unashamed." Meanwhile, literary critic Edmund Wilson famously criticized The Lord of the Rings in a review published in *The Nation*. In his article titled "Oo, Those Awful Orcs!" he claimed that the people who enjoyed Tolkien's trilogy "have a lifelong appetite for juvenile trash." And critic Philip Toynbee wrote in a later review in *The Observer* that "even the most devoted admirers of Tolkien must surely admit that the books are dull, ill-written, and wearisome."

In the literary world of Tolkien's time, readers desired a different take, but Tolkien's work would gain a kind of cult following that eventually made his popularity skyrocket—especially as his books caught the eye of Americans.

LITERARY CONNECTIONS

While J.R.R. Tolkien spent a number of years working on his fantasy epic, his dear friend C.S. Lewis managed to rush through the publication of his most well-known work: The Chronicles of Narnia. The seven books in this series only took Lewis about five years to write, as opposed to the twelve years Tolkien spent writing The Lord of the Rings trilogy.

J.R.R. Tolkien, the Illustrator

Despite mostly being known as an author, J.R.R. Tolkien was also a visual artist! His mother, Mabel, taught him the skill early in life, and many of the maps and drawings found in the early editions of *The Hobbit* and The Lord of the Rings were created by Tolkien himself. Ten of his illustrations made their way into the very first edition of *The Hobbit*, including the now-famous idealized version of the hobbit homelands titled *The Hill: Hobbiton-across-the-Water*, which depicts the landscape of Bag End and the surrounding countryside. As Tolkien scholar Humphrey Carpenter notes in *J.R.R. Tolkien: A Biography*, The Professor "had never entirely abandoned this childhood hobby, and during his undergraduate days he illustrated several of his own poems."

An entire book titled *Pictures by J.R.R. Tolkien* features forty-eight different drawings by The Professor. Tolkien was enamored with large structures and quaint hobbit homes, and his drawings include the Doors of Durin where the fellowship enter the Mines of Moria; Orthanc, the impenetrable tower controlled by Saruman; and Helm's Deep, where the Battle of the Hornburg took place between Théoden's forces and the evil orcs. Then there are Tolkien's maps. *The Hobbit* features two of his maps: One is Thror's map of the

Lonely Mountain, which he passed down to his son, Thorin Oakenshield. The other is a map of Wilderland, or Rhovanion, encompassing the vast forest of Mirkwood. Between these two maps, only about fifty different places are named. The Lord of the Rings, however, features three maps showing over six hundred different locations. In a letter to writer Naomi Mitchison, Tolkien said of The Lord of the Rings, "I wisely started with a map, and made the story fit (generally with meticulous care for distances)."

The More You Know

In 2022, the Tolkien Estate made a selection of Tolkien's art available on their website, www.tolkienestate.com. This includes some artwork from The Lord of the Rings, as well as visual works outside Tolkien's legendarium. The collection also features previously unpublished items, including some Tolkien family photos and paintings of exotic birds and flowers.

But Wait, There's More

The Lord of the Rings has had many adaptations. The first (a radio adaptation) came in 1955, the same year *The Return of the King* was first published.

Just to name a few, there are two radio adaptations (between 1955 and 1981), one three-and-a-half-hour musical theater production in 2006 (the musical was trimmed down to three hours for a 2007 revival), an early-2000s movie trilogy that won seventeen Academy Awards (more on these films later!), and a 1985 Soviet-era television play in which the fellowship uses Gimli as a table to look at a map. That isn't even counting the video games inspired by Tolkien's works—there are over twenty-five of those. (About a dozen of them are based off the trilogy of films directed by Peter Jackson.)

The Lord of the Rings itself is presented by Tolkien as an adaptation. In the trilogy, Frodo inherits the *Red Book of Westmarch*, the red leather-bound book where Bilbo wrote about his adventures (the same adventures detailed in *The Hobbit*). Bilbo eventually passed the book—originally a personal diary—on to his heir, Frodo, who organizes the stories and documents his own quest to destroy the One Ring in The Lord of the Rings. Tolkien's attempt at "translating" or "adapting" their story is particularly notable to fans and Tolkien scholars, considering his many misgivings about adaptations of his work (more on this later).

LITERARY CONNECTIONS

The inspiration for Bilbo's, and eventually Frodo's, narratives of their adventures, the *Red Book of Westmarch*, stems from the *Mabinogion*, a compilation of Welsh stories from the fifteenth century that is, coincidentally, also bound in red leather. Because this book, which Tolkien described as a treasure of Medieval Welsh, was housed at the Bodleian Library at Oxford, Tolkien had access to it.

From The Two Towers, "The Stairs of Cirith Ungol"

"I wonder if we shall ever be put into songs or tales. We're in one, of course; but I mean: put into words, you know, told by the fireside, or read out of a great big book with red and black letters, years and years afterwards. And people will say: 'Let's hear about Frodo and the Ring!' And they'll say: 'Yes, that's one of my favourite stories. Frodo was very brave, wasn't he, dad?' 'Yes, my boy, the famousest of the hobbits, and that's saying a lot.'"

—Samwise Gamgee

Human Stories

J.R.R. Tolkien was surrounded by death and grief for most of his life. The loss of his father and mother and his many close friends during and soon after World War I fundamentally shaped the way he perceived death and grief, and how he wrote about it in his stories. Making it all worse was the constant threat of death during the Second World War. Whether it was his children fighting overseas in this war or his and Edith's well-being at home, Tolkien's expression of that grief went on the page. In The Lord of the Rings, specifically, it started to take the form of Anglo-Saxon poetry.

In *The Two Towers*, Aragorn recites a poem of the founder of Rohan, Eorl the Young, and his horse, Felaróf. The first two lines, "Where now the horse and the rider? Where is the horn that was blowing?" are taken from an Old English poem known as *The Wanderer*. The original poem can be found in 115 lines from the *Exeter Book*, a manuscript dating back to the tenth century. It tells the story of a warrior as he wanders the world in grief after the loss of his people.

Yet death is not always meant to convey just grief. The god of the legendarium Eru gives humans what is called "The Gift of Men." The gift itself is to die—to continue on past those of even the elves and the dwarves. Tolkien actually discusses the concept of death in a 1968 BBC documentary titled *Tolkien in Oxford*. In it, he notes that "human stories are always about one thing—death. The inevitability of death."

THE MORE YOU KNOW

During World War I, Tolkien's brothers-in-arms in the Lancashire Fusiliers earned a total of eighteen Victoria Crosses—more than any other British infantry regiment. Established in 1856, the Victoria Cross is awarded to those who show gallantry in the face of the enemy, as Tolkien's fellow soldiers did during this influential and difficult time in his life.

This Faramir Fellow

In *The Two Towers,* Tolkien introduces the character of Faramir, brother of Boromir of Gondor. Of all the characters in The Lord of the Rings legendarium, J.R.R Tolkien considered Faramir to be the most like himself, though Tolkien discovered Faramir entirely by accident: "A new character has come on the scene. (I am sure I did not invent him, I did not even want him, though I like him . . .)." Faramir first appears in Book 2 of *The Two Towers,* in the chapter called "Of Herbs and Stewed Rabbit," though the first mention of him in the trilogy happens much earlier, in *The Fellowship of the Ring* when Boromir mentions him during the Council of Elrond.

Faramir is the embodiment of loyalty and strength. "I do not love the bright sword for its sharpness," says Faramir to the two hobbits Frodo and Sam in *The Two Towers,* "nor the arrow for its swiftness, nor the warrior for his glory. I love only that which they defend." Faramir also provides a sharp contrast to the effects of the One Ring on human beings. His brother, Boromir, falls to the temptation of the One Ring, but Faramir does not. Knowing how his brother was tempted by the ring and that the ring is inherently evil, Faramir tells Frodo that even if he could use the ring to save Minis Tirith, he would not choose to do so.

LITERARY CONNECTIONS

A decent portion of the book's scenes involving Faramir were almost relegated to the appendices in *Return of the King*. In a letter to Christopher Tolkien, he mentions that writing Faramir was taking more time than usual: " . . . if he goes on much more a lot of him will have to be removed to the appendices—where some fascinating material on the hobbit Tobacco industry and the Language of the West have gone."

From The Two Towers (Peregrin Took)

Here was one with an air of high nobility such as Aragorn at times revealed, less high perhaps, yet also less incalculable and remote: one of the Kings of Men born into a later time, but touched with the wisdom and sadness of the Eldar. He knew now why Beregond spoke his name with love. He was a captain that men would follow, that he would follow, even under the shadow of the black wings.

Atlantis Is Waiting

Within the legendarium of J.R.R. Tolkien are numerous kingdoms of elves, dwarves, and humans. But only one is swallowed up by the sea—in a great tidal wave hinted at briefly by Faramir in *The Two Towers*. He tells of a dream he often has of a "great dark wave climbing over green lands and above the hills, and coming on, darkness unescapable."

Tolkien later admitted that he had the same recurring dream: "This legend or myth or dim memory of some ancient history has always troubled me. In sleep I had the dreadful dream of the ineluctable Wave, either coming out of the quiet sea, or coming in towering over the green inlands. It still occurs occasionally, though now exorcized by writing about it. It always ends by surrender, and I awake gasping out of deep water. I used to draw it or write bad poems about it."

This wave would eventually wipe out the fictional island of Númenor, the greatest of human kingdoms in Tolkien's legendarium. Its inhabitants lived on a kind of island utopia just off the coast of Middle-earth. The island of Númenor acts as Tolkien's own version of Atlantis, the mythical island first mentioned by the philosopher Plato. The legend of Atlantis tells of an advanced society that ruled over much of the world until the island was sunk by gods because its people became greedy. In Tolkien's version of the story, the humans who lived on Númenor had almost superhuman powers: They were taller than other humans, lived for hundreds of years, and had the resources to establish themselves as a military power of Middle-earth. It wasn't just the people of Númenor that were superhuman; some of the animals were too. In Tompollë, in the region of Númenor called Forostar, there was an autumn event known as Ruxotompalë, in which a group of as many as fifty bears performed intricate dances with: "slow and dignified grace."

LITERARY CONNECTIONS

Despite Númenor's eventual sinking into the ocean, the tradition of the Great Bear-dance lived on. In the chapter "Queer Lodgings" in *The Hobbit*, Bilbo, Gandalf, Thorin, and company stay at the home of the bear/human skin-changer Beorn, and Gandalf remarks: "I should say there were little bears, large bears, ordinary bears, and gigantic big bears, all dancing outside from dark to nearly dawn."

The people on the island kingdom of Númenor became corrupted thanks in large part to Sauron, who was taken as a prisoner by Númenóreans. A civil war, Sauron's manipulation, and the pride of kings led to Númenor's downfall; the island eventually sank into the ocean after the "great wave" wiped it out. The few who survived and escaped became the kings of Middle-earth.

In a letter to a fan sent in 1961, Tolkien explained that the name Númenor came from the compound of the Quenya Elvish words *numē-n,* meaning "going down, sunset, West," and *nōrë,* meaning "land" (specifically land with a particular people in it). So "Númenor" literally translates to "Westlands" or "Westernesse."

The Undying Lands & Other Bizarre Geography

One of the final scenes in *The Return of the King* finds Frodo, Bilbo, Gandalf, Galadriel, and Elrond sailing to the Undying Lands. To many scholars, this voyage represents a kind of passing away or a symbolic journey to heaven. This is partially true, but in exploring his father's writings after his death, Christopher Tolkien gave the public an entirely new interpretation of what it meant to sail "into the West."

According to the Tolkien legendarium, the world containing the continents of Middle-earth and the Undying Lands was originally flat until being made round by the creator god, Eru Ilúvatar. (This happened at the same time the tidal wave sank Númenor.) Thanks to a giant icy tundra connecting the two, elves once crossed from the Undying Lands to Middle-earth, though the journey claimed many elven lives and soon became impossible. When Eru made the world round, he moved the Undying Lands out of reach except by the Straight Road, which could only be navigated by elves. Scholars have often pointed to parallels between the Straight Road and the Bifröst found in Norse mythology.

Once through the Straight Road, Frodo would have found himself on the island off the coast of the Undying Lands, also known as Aman. A symbolic yet also literal heaven on earth, Aman is a paradise of enormous trees, mountains, and golden fields of grain and impossible beauty that heals elves (and a few hobbits as well) who've grown weary of Middle-earth.

LITERARY CONNECTIONS

The Undying Lands, as they are known in Middle-earth, share many parallels to other lands of paradise in folklore and mythology. After his final battle, King Arthur of Camelot is eventually taken to the magical island of Avalon. And in Irish mythology, the island of Tír na nÓg (Land of the Young) is an island paradise of everlasting youth.

The Appendices

One thing J.R.R. Tolkien never struggled with was reaching the necessary word count for his books. Though sometimes passed over by readers, the appendices found at the end of *The Return of the King* provide an incredibly rich and detailed look at just how much of the story there was left to tell after The Lord of the Rings ended. Broken up into six parts (Appendices A through F), they present a thorough description of the events and the actions of characters before, during, and after the events of the trilogy. The ancestral record of kings and rulers in Appendix A is almost a history in itself, detailing the royal lines for Númenor, Rohan, and Gondor. And that's not to mention the detailed genealogies provided for the Baggins, Took, and Brandybuck families of the Shire! Material from *Unfinished Tales*, like "The Quest for Erebor" and "The Hunt for the Ring," was written for these appendices as well but was ultimately excluded due to space issues.

Also found in the appendices is a calendar giving the exact dates of events of the trilogy. Tolkien even included timelines for events of all of the ages, from the First through the Fourth Age after Aragorn is crowned king. The Tengwar script for the Elves and the Cirth runes for the dwarves appear in an appendix as well, along with the pronunciations of words and names.

The amount of world building in these pages was unlike that for any other book published at the time. It thoroughly bridged the gap between the events of The Lord of the Rings and the earlier events of *The Silmarillion* in the First and Second Ages (despite *The Silmarillion* not yet being published).

LITERARY CONNECTIONS

In 1968, Tolkien's publisher, Allen & Unwin, printed *The Tale of Aragorn and Arwen,* typically found in Appendix A of *The Return of the King,* as a single-volume paperback book. This book gives readers the history behind the epic love story of the mysterious Ranger and his elven love from their first meeting until their deaths.

"It's Your Sam"

In March 1956, Tolkien received a letter from a man named Samwise Gamgee. Gamgee (the real-life person) had heard his name said in 1955 on a BBC Radio adaptation of The Lord of the Rings. He later wrote to Tolkien, "I was rather interested at how you arrived at the name of one of the characters named Sam Gamgee because that happens to be my name." Tolkien was delighted. "You can imagine my astonishment," said The Professor in his return letter to Gamgee, "when I saw your signature!"

Samwise Gamgee is one of the most recognizable names in twentieth-century literature. In a letter to Milton Walden, Tolkien even refers to this humble gardener as "the chief hero" of The Lord of the Rings. At first sent by Gandalf to accompany Frodo to the human city of Bree, Samwise Gamgee eventually finds himself in Mordor, playing a crucial role in destroying the One Ring.

It was Tolkien's love of Anglo-Saxon that came into play in naming this character: The Anglo-Saxon prefix "sam" means "half," suggesting that Samwise is only "half-wise." His name, then, suggests that he is somewhat foolish, and Tolkien meant it to be this way. Through the hero of Samwise, Tolkien created a kind of everyday person—someone that readers of any age could see themselves in. According to Tolkien, he also used the character of Sam "[p]recisely to bring out the comicness, peasantry, and if you will the Englishry of this jewel among the hobbits."

LITERARY CONNECTIONS

In The Lord of The Rings, the Ents and Entwives operated under different beliefs. Whereas the Ents wished to let the trees grow how they pleased, the Entwives desired order and wished to be obeyed by plants.

Good versus Evil

One of the themes most consistently found in The Lord of the Rings (in fact, across Tolkien's entire legendarium) is the eternal battle of good versus evil. His own Roman Catholic belief in the constant battle between God and the devil helped shape his literary works. In Tolkien's mind, good and evil are in direct opposition to each other but are not equal: Because of his own understanding of evil, good is far more powerful than evil in his works. As Frodo says to Sam about orcs: "The Shadow that bred them can only mock, it cannot make: not real new things of its own. I don't think it gave life to the orcs, it only ruined them and twisted them."

Evil, in Tolkien's view, is a kind of corruption that can (and often does) affect anything: "For nothing is evil in the beginning. Even Sauron was not so." Before he attempted to cover Middle-earth in a second darkness, Sauron was a powerful being on the side of good. As was Saruman the White—before his curiosity grew to an obsession for power. Even Saruman's henchman, Gríma Wormtongue, was a man of Rohan before he tried to corrupt Theoden's mind. And Gollum was an ordinary hobbit before the One Ring took over his mind for five hundred years. Yet, in Tolkien's mind, there was always hope of redemption from this corruption. This is seen most clearly when Boromir's fall to the One Ring's temptation is later redeemed as he sacrifices his life to try to save the hobbits Merry and Pippin.

LITERARY CONNECTIONS

Gandalf was the only one of five wizards to fulfill their task of helping the people of Middle-earth defeat Sauron. Saruman fell into darkness and Radagast did not take part in the quest to destroy the ring. The other two wizards, Alatar and Pallando, went through several iterations of characterization, but their stories were never finalized during Tolkien's lifetime.

From The Two Towers Film Adaptation

"But in the end, it's only a passing thing, this shadow. Even darkness must pass. A new day will come. And when the sun shines it will shine out the clearer. I know now folks in those stories had lots of chances of turning back, only they didn't. They kept going because they were holding on to something. That there's some good in this world, Mr. Frodo, and it's worth fighting for."

—Samwise Gamgee

The Many Languages of The Lord of the Rings and Beyond

Crucial not just to The Lord of the Rings but to many of J.R.R. Tolkien's works was his love of languages. He developed at least fifteen different languages, beginning in 1910 with Elvish (explored earlier in this book), and he continued making revisions to the language until his death. Among the most fleshed-out Tolkien languages are:

- Westron: Known as the Common Speech, a default language in Middle-earth.
- Quenya: One of the two elven languages. It is spoken by the High Elves.
- Sindarin: The second of the two elven languages. This is the form of Elvish you hear most often in the Peter Jackson films as well as *The Rings of Power* television show.
- Khuzdûl: The language spoken by the dwarves of Middle-earth.
- Adûnaic: The language spoken by the people of Númenor, the island between Middle-earth and the Undying Lands.

- Entish: The language created for the sentient tree guardians, the Ents.
- Black Speech: The language used in Mordor by orcs and the Nazgûl. It is also the language used for the inscription found on the One Ring.
- Rohanese: The language spoken by the folk of Rohan, though often referred to as Rohirric by fans.

The language element of Tolkien's works gets even more complicated when it comes to character names. In fact, popular characters like Frodo Baggins have different "real names." Frodo's real name is actually Maura Labingi when translated into Westron. Westron, as previously mentioned, is the language most commonly spoken by the peoples of Middle-earth, including by hobbits. This goes back to Tolkien's narrative of events in Middle-earth being originally written by the fictional characters Bilbo and Frodo Baggins—a kind of meta-fictional history.

LITERARY CONNECTIONS

Other character names in Westron include:

Bilbo Baggins—Bilba Labingi
Samwise Gamgee—Banazîr Galpsi
Peregrine Took—Razanur Tûk
Meriadoc Brandybuck—Kalimac Brandagamba

Illustrators of Middle-earth

Of the fifty-seven languages The Lord of the Rings has been translated into, the Danish version of The Lord of the Rings is the only one to be illustrated by a queen—though very few people actually knew the queen was doing any kind of illustrating at the time. Queen Margrethe II, born April 16, 1940 (just a week after the Nazis invaded Denmark), reigned for exactly fifty-two years as the queen of Denmark. She ascended to the throne after the death of her father, Frederik IX, on January 14, 1972, and abdicated on January 14, 2024. Among the many tasks she handled as a monarch, Queen Margrethe II used her skills as an artist to illustrate the Danish translation of The Lord of the Rings, under the pseudonym Ingahild Grathmer in 1977.

Long before the technology existed to bring Gollum to life on the silver screen in The Lord of the Rings movie trilogy, the character of Gollum loomed 15 feet tall for many fans of Tolkien's books. This was thanks to Finnish author and illustrator Tove Jansson. Creator of the beloved troll characters known as Moomins, Jansson was left with quite the impression when she first read *The Hobbit*, and she later created her own interpretation of Gollum for the Swedish translation of the book in 1962. The image looks like something out of gothic horror. In his biography of Jansson, Paul Gravett described her depiction: "Her Gollum towered monstrously large, to the surprise of Tolkien himself, who realized that he had never clarified Gollum's size and so amended the second edition to describe him as 'a small slimy creature.'"

In one of Jansson's illustrations for *The Hobbit*, Bilbo stands with his sword, Sting, at the ready on the shores of a lake deep within a cavern and Gollum stands waist deep in the middle of that lake. With his eyes the size of dinner plates and a crown of flowers on his head, much of his wide face is shrouded in shadow.

LITERARY CONNECTIONS

Scholar Douglas A. Anderson suggests the name Gollum comes from an Old Norse root word for gold: *goll*.

Tolkien and His Readers

J.R.R. Tolkien wrote hundreds of letters to people throughout his life—and they continue to be one of the most influential primary sources when it comes to Middle-earth. Many of the original typed or handwritten letters have sold for quite a lot of money at auction. Fans and scholars consider them treasures of literary history and believe there are more letters out there that haven't yet been found or shared with the public. (Much more on Tolkien's letters later.)

Tolkien spent a lot of time answering fan mail over the course of his career, and, according to scholar Humphrey Carpenter, he "took every letter seriously. Especially if it came from a child or elderly person." A little over ten years after *The Hobbit* was published, he exchanged letters with a young reader named Hugh Brogan. After Brogan first reached out in 1948 to praise *The Hobbit* and ask if Tolkien was writing another book set in Middle-earth, Tolkien replied: "I hope at least to finish it this year, and will certainly let you have advance information." And Tolkien did write back to Brogan in October of that year to say he had finished The Lord of the Rings. The two continued to send letters back and forth over the course of the next few years, with the last known letter from Tolkien to Brogan dated 1956. In this final letter, Tolkien invited Brogan to meet him, comparing his visit to "returning to the shire."

Tolkien was known to be a witty and deeply humorous man at most times, yet his fame puzzled him. He was thrilled that readers were enthusiastic about the world he had created and continued to write about. But soon things got tiresome. His private address had been made public, and his telephone number could be found in the Oxford directory; the phone would ring at all hours, and some people even showed up at his house without an appointment asking for an autograph or money.

LITERARY CONNECTIONS

While J.R.R. Tolkien generally accepted gifts from fans, he was not always thrilled with the gifts he received. In a letter to author and editor Sterling Lanier, he described one such gift: "I had a similar disappointment when a drinking goblet arrived (from a fan) which proved to be of steel engraved with the terrible words seen on the Ring. I of course have never drunk from it, but use it for tobacco ash."

"Questions That Need Answering"

For as many answers as Tolkien gave his readers about Middle-earth, there are quite a few questions he left unanswered when he finally published *The Return of the King* in 1955. Readers would wait more than twenty years for any new information. In a letter to Milton Waldman, who almost published The Lord of the Rings books, Tolkien remarked, "I would draw some of the great tales in fullness, and leave many only placed in the scheme and sketched. The cycles should be linked to a majestic whole, and yet leave scope for other minds and hands, wielding paint and music and drama." Christopher Tolkien helped answer many of those questions when he published *The Silmarillion* in 1977.

But even with the depth of the lore he created and the publication of *The Silmarillion*, J.R.R. Tolkien left many questions about his universe unresolved. So, in 1981, twenty-six years after *The Return of the King* first hit bookshelves, Allen & Unwin published *The Letters of J.R.R. Tolkien*, edited by Humphrey Carpenter and Christopher Tolkien. This first edition had a total of 354 letters; the second edition released in 2023 added 154 more. With the publication of these letters, many questions that had been left to the reader's imagination were finally answered.

It seemed that Tolkien couldn't help but answer when a fan wrote to him with a question about something in his legendarium. "Where did the entwives go?," Oxford colleague Naomi Mitchison inquired of Tolkien. He responded in part of a seven-page letter: "I think that in fact the Entwives had disappeared for good, being destroyed with their gardens in the War of the Last Alliance . . . when Sauron pursued a scorched earth policy and burned their lands." And a fan named Rhona Beare wrote to ask him, "What were the colours of the two wizards mentioned but not named in the book?" (The fact that there were five wizards sent to Middle-earth is only briefly noted by Saruman in *The Two Towers* when he mentions the "rods of the Five Wizards.") Tolkien replied, "I really do not know anything clearly about the other two—since they do not concern the history of the N.W. I think they went as emissaries to distant regions, East and South, far out of Númenórean range. . . . What success they had I do not know; but I fear that they failed." When asked for a "brief sketch" of how *The Silmarillion* connected to The Lord of the Rings, Tolkien responded with a ten thousand–word letter that started, "The attempt to say a few words opens a floodgate of excitement . . . "

Literary Connections

Smaug the dragon, as he is depicted in the Peter Jackson Hobbit trilogy, is not a dragon at all, but a wyvern. Traditional imagery of a dragon in Western cultures depict dragons as having four legs and two wings; six limbs total. A wyvern is traditionally accepted as having only four limbs, with the wings attached to the front two limbs—which is the case for Smaug in the Jackson trilogy. Tolkien made an illustration of Smaug, called "Conversation with Smaug," that depicts the creature as having six limbs and sitting on a pile of gold.

From The Return of the King

There, peeping among the cloud-wrack above a dark tor high up in the mountains, Sam saw a white star twinkle for a while. The beauty of it smote his heart, as he looked up out of the forsaken land, and hope returned to him. For like a shaft, clear and cold, the thought pierced him that in the end the Shadow was only a small and passing thing: there was a light and high beauty for ever beyond its reach. His song in the Tower had been defiance rather than hope; for then he was thinking of himself. Now, for a moment, his own fate, and even his master's, ceased to trouble him. He crawled back into the brambles and laid himself by Frodo's side, and putting away all fear he cast himself into a deep untroubled sleep.

The Band Down the Road

Readers weren't the only ones getting in on the adventure and creativity of The Lord of The Rings! In the 1960s, in the wake of what was called Beatlemania (a kind of fan frenzy surrounding the popular British rock and roll group), none other than the Beatles themselves discussed making a Lord of the Rings musical film. Between news reports and television appearances on popular programs like *The Ed Sullivan Show*, these four musicians had a profound impact on the entertainment industry. In the midst of their success and fame, British film producer Denis O'Dell suggested the group star in an adaptation of The Lord of the Rings. The Beatles had already starred in two movies, *A Hard Day's Night* (also produced by O'Dell) and *Help!*, and were contracted to film a third. To O'Dell and the band, it seemed like a great idea.

The More You Know

The Beatles each had a role in mind for the proposed musical film of The Lord of the Rings. John Lennon wanted to play Gandalf, but he changed his mind and decided to play Frodo instead. However, that role was already seen as Paul McCartney's. Paul later told Peter Jackson that Ringo Starr would play Sam, John Lennon would play Gollum, and George Harrison would play Gandalf, with musician Donovan in the role of Merry and actress/model Twiggy to join the cast as Galadriel.

Plans were put in place, spearheaded by John Lennon, who wanted director Stanley Kubrick to helm the film. But things quickly started to fall through. As O'Dell later noted in his book *At the Apple's Core: The Beatles from the Inside,* Kubrick said no to the movie, believing the books to be unfilmable. The Beatles, who were massive fans of the books, then went to the author himself; they were staying in Liverpool at the time, just a few hours' drive from Tolkien's Oxford home. But like Kubrick, Tolkien said no. Why would one of the most successful authors of modern fantasy turn down a collaboration with the biggest musicians of the time? He didn't like their genre of music. In a letter to his son Christopher, Tolkien describes his displeasure at the music coming from his neighborhood: "[I]n a house three doors away dwells a member of a group of young men who are evidently aiming to turn themselves into a Beatle Group. On days when it falls to his turn to have a practice session the noise is indescribable."

Despite the Beatles' efforts, the musical film was ultimately abandoned, although Tolkien's books would continue to inspire the music industry for years to come.

Tolkien-Inspired Music

Music and poetry feature heavily in The Lord of the Rings trilogy, so much so that there is an album called *Complete Songs and Poems*: a nearly four-hour-long compilation of all sixty-nine of the songs and poems featured in the books set to music. Some of the most well-known musical artists of their time have referenced Tolkien's works. The iconic rock and roll band Led Zeppelin mentions both Mordor and Gollum in their 1969 song "Ramble On." And Black Sabbath's song "The Wizard" is inspired partly by Gandalf, as it features an old man in a "Long grey cloak." The list goes on: The band Rush has a song called "Rivendell," and British progressive rock band Camel has a multipart song over nine minutes long called "Nimrodel/Procession/White Rider" that features an ode to Gandalf as they sing of his fall against the evil balrog.

Entire albums have been dedicated to *The Silmarillion*. German metal band Blind Guardian composed their album *Nightfall in Middle-Earth* as an ode to *The Silmarillion* in 1998. Filled with spoken dialogue, numerous heavy metal songs, and an operatic approach to progressive rock, it has cemented itself as one of the band's most popular albums. But perhaps the most well-known Tolkien-related music comes from those composing The Professor's songs into their own arrangements. Clamavi De Profundis, which translates to "I cried out from the depths" is a musical group (and real-life family) that was inspired by Tolkien's works and have put his poems to a tune. The group's top ten songs currently have over 155 million views on YouTube.

Even some band names have been lifted directly from Tolkien's legendarium. Over thirty different bands are on record taking names from Middle-earth, including Amon Amarth, Cirith Ungol, and Rivendell (a musical project previously named Fangorn).

The More You Know

There is even a subgenre of black metal music called Tolkien metal that features lyrics about his work. The Austrian band Summoning are at the forefront of the genre, and their most recent album (released in 2018) features the songs "Carcharoth" and "With Doom I Come"—both of which drew inspiration from Tolkien's poem *The Lay of Leithian*.

The Ace Paperbacks

J.R.R. Tolkien hated paperback books. He considered them to be the "degenerate form" of a book. Among the many editions of The Lord of the Rings, the very first paperbacks ever published were done so illegally!

Copyright laws (especially international copyright laws) of the 1950s and 1960s were fairly complex and sometimes easy to exploit, and exploited they were. Tolkien's original publishers, Allen & Unwin, did not properly renew the copyright protection for the editions of The Lord of the Rings sold in the United States by Houghton Mifflin. So, the American company Ace Books, headed by Donald A. Wollheim and A.A. Wyn, printed the trilogy as unauthorized paperbacks in July 1965.

This was not the first time Ace Books had tried to publish The Lord of the Rings. They had previously reached out to Tolkien about a paperback edition. Tolkien refused on principal. Ace did it anyway: Using a loophole in the public domain laws, Ace sold the first paperback edition of the work. The unauthorized 1965 printings cost just 75 cents per book, and sold more than 100,000 copies. Tolkien was furious: "I have been taken off all my other work and driven nearly over the edge by the attempt to get an *authorized* paperback," he wrote to Nan C. Scott. Scott was a fan and, according to Christopher Tolkien, also the lead campaigner in "the battle to keep the pirate edition of The Lord of the Rings out of American bookshops."

Tolkien got to work on a revised version of The Lord of the Rings, and gave the US publisher Ballantine Books his approval to publish these new versions in America. A new foreword and index, revisions to the appendices, and an extended prologue made up most of the revisions. Also present at the very beginning of the book was a note to readers that made it clear how The Professor felt about the Ace paperbacks: "This paperback edition, and no other, has been published with my consent and cooperation. Those who approve of courtesy (at least) to living authors will purchase it and no other." Ballantine Books sold more than 125,000 copies of each volume. Ace would eventually stop printing their editions of the trilogy and agree to pay Tolkien back royalties. Copies of this pirated paperback are still for sale, however. And Tolkien later said that at least the Ace edition book covers represented elements of the books—something that he did not feel about the Ballantine edition covers.

The More You Know

The Lord of the Rings will not enter the public domain until 2044. The copyright for all things Tolkien is directly handled by the Tolkien Estate, the legal body that manages the rights and distribution of the works of J.R.R. Tolkien.

Tolkien As a Counterculture Icon

The rise of industrialization across the globe, the constant threat of war, and countercultural movements were all happening at just the right time for a professor from England to make his mark on the world. A 1968 article in *The Telegraph* noted: "He is also a literary opiate for hippies, who carry his works to their farthest-flung pads, from San Francisco to Istanbul and Nepal."

The release of the more affordable paperback editions of The Lord of the Rings allowed J.R.R. Tolkien's trilogy to reach a much wider fan base. Even a decade after the books were published, they were still gaining popularity. The Professor's idealized world with simple yet three-dimensional characters fighting an oppressive force of evil and mechanization was exactly the world that people wanted to imaginatively enter into at the time. The phrase "Frodo Lives" was graffitied around numerous college campuses, as well as plastered on bumper stickers, T-shirts, and buttons!

By the 1970s, Tolkien was so popular, he couldn't believe it. In a letter to Christopher, Tolkien provided a glimpse into just how well his books were selling at the time: "'Accountancy' told me that the sales of *The Hobbit* were now rocketing up to hitherto unreached heights. Also a large order of copies of *The L.R.* had just come in. When I did not show quite the gratified surprise expected I was gently told that a single order of 100 copies used to be pleasing . . . but this one for *The L.R.* was for 6,000." The estimated total for combined sales of all three Lord of the Rings books and *The Hobbit* is now estimated to be over 250 million copies worldwide.

THE MORE YOU KNOW

Tolkien's love of nature and his experiences in war heavily influenced both his writing and the reception of his works amid the chaos of the 1960s. Tolkien's worldview resonated with civil rights activists, hippies, those protesting the Vietnam War, and anyone who wanted to change the status quo.

The Sequel That Never Was

After the success of The Lord of the Rings trilogy, it seemed only natural to the literary community that Tolkien should write a sequel. Tolkien did try to write a story that went beyond the Third Age of Middle-earth, but scholars believe that his heart lay in the tales of the First Age. Eventually, pen met paper, but Tolkien judged the resulting story "sinister and depressing."

The sequel was supposed to be called *The New Shadow*. The titular "shadow" is an evil that arises nearly one hundred years after the events of The Lord of the Rings. Aragorn's son, Eldarion, is now king, and this evil is rising in Middle-earth. Humans, such as Tolkien viewed them, were inherently flawed creatures constantly falling back into their selfish behaviors. Anger, greed, and selfishness plague Minas Tirith, and the sequel to The Lord of the Rings trilogy meant to explore these aspects of human nature.

A human named Borlas opens the story. Borlas is the son of Beregond, a character readers first met in *The Return of the King.* While in his garden, Borlas speaks to a young man named Saelon about the evil that still lurks in the hearts of men. There is also mention of ships disappearing along the river Anduin.

Though optimism is almost always somewhere to be found in each chapter of Tolkien's legendarium, he considered it inevitable that human beings would fall prey to evil, and the characters of the sequel would be no exception. As history so often repeats itself in the real world, so, too, did Tolkien see it happen in the world of Middle-earth: "while the dynasts descended from Aragorn would become just kings and governors—like Denethor or worse."

Not going any further than an initial scene that spans thirteen pages, *The New Shadow* offers a kind of "what if" scenario that extends the history of Middle-earth beyond the appendices. As has been the case with some other fantasy worlds found in popular works, the sequel as it exists does not feel quite as satisfying. It does, however, give readers a unique insight into Tolkien's views on the persistence of evil despite the many dark lords of the realm suffering multiple defeats.

THE MORE YOU KNOW

Tolkien discussed his ill-fated sequel to The Lord of the Rings just fifteen months before his death. He noted in a letter that a time of peace after overthrowing Sauron would have little interest to readers as well as the characters in the tale, leading to notions of secret evil societies and the forming of "orc-cults" among adolescents.

From The New Shadow

This tale begins in the days of Eldarion, son of that Elessar of whom the histories have much to tell. One hundred and five years had passed since the fall of the Dark Tower, and the story of that time was little heeded now by most of the people of Gondor, though a few were still living who could remember the War of the Ring as a shadow upon their early childhood.

Smith of Wootton Major

As The Lord of The Rings continued to grow in popularity, J.R.R. Tolkien published a tale, *Smith of Wootton Major*, in 1967. Considered to be quintessentially Tolkien, this allegorical work combines The Professor's love of both the mortal world and the magical realms of his imagination. In the story, a grand feast is held every twenty-four years in the village of Wootton Major. The newly appointed Master Cook prepares a cake for the feast and fills it with small surprises (thought by some to be an ode to the hobbits of Middle-earth giving away gifts on their own birthdays). This particular feast and the aftermath cause quite a stir for the main character, a young boy named Smith.

The current Master Cook, Nokes, finds a silver star, but not knowing the star's significance, bakes it into the cake. Smith, a nine-year-old boy, eats the silver star and gains the ability to enter into the magical realm of Faery. But before long, the star Smith ate must be passed on to someone else:

> "Do you not think, Master Smith," said Alf, "that it is time for you to give this thing [the silver star] up?"

> "What is that to you, Master Cook?" he answered. "And why should I do so? Isn't it mine? It came to me, and may a man not keep things that come to him so, at least as a remembrance?"
>
> "Some things. Those that are free gifts and given for remembrance. But others are not so given. They cannot belong to a man for ever, nor be treasured as heirlooms. They are lent."

This deeply reflective story highlights the fascination Tolkien had with Faery and with myth. Focusing on themes of tradition with the grand feast, and symbolizing the world of magic with the silver star, Tolkien captures his own desire to exist within the world of the fae while often being needed elsewhere.

LITERARY CONNECTIONS

J.R.R. Tolkien created his own version of a deus ex machina ("day-uus EX mak-eena"), or "God from the machine," a literary device originating in Greek times to end plays. In a deus ex machina, a problem is solved by an unexpected person or occurrence. Tolkien, however, created his own phrase for it in *The Silmarillion*: "For he that attempteth this shall prove but mine instrument in the devising of things more wonderful"—"shall prove but mine instrument" caught on as a kind of catchphrase among Tolkien fans and is lovingly referred to as SPBMI (pronounced "spuh-BIM-ee").

From Smith of Wootton Major

Far off there was a great hill of shadow, and out of that shadow, which was its root, he saw the King's Tree springing up, tower upon tower, into the sky, and its light was like the sun at noon; and it bore at once leaves and flowers and fruits uncounted, and not one was the same as any other that grew on The Tree.

Edith's Passing

As Edith Tolkien grew older, she suffered from a lameness caused by arthritis. But she continued to be the homemaker for many years. At one point in 1962, Jane Neave, Tolkien's aunt, wrote to them apparently suggesting she would return money Tolkien had gifted her so he could buy Edith a wheelchair. Tolkien refused. "We should have to reorganize life altogether if she was reduced to a chair!," he wrote to Neave in the letter. "She does all the cooking, most of the housework, and some of the gardening." But old age had caught up with them, and the life Tolkien had known for the past fifty-five years was about to change forever. In mid-November of 1971, Edith became sick with an inflamed gallbladder and was taken to the hospital. She would not return home.

Edith Tolkien died on Monday, November 29, 1971. Daughter of Frances Bratt and Alfred Warrilow; wife to J.R.R. Tolkien for fifty-five years; and the mother of their four children John, Michael, Christopher, and Priscilla; she was eighty-two years old. She is buried at Wolvercote Cemetery in Oxford. In their time together boarding at the same house, Edith and John Ronald "became allies against 'the Old Lady,'" as they called Mrs. Faulkner, and their bond would carry on for half a century.

Tolkien deeply mourned Edith after she passed in 1971. By the few correspondences he made during that time in his life, he was inconsolable. "I am afflicted from time to time (increasingly) with an overwhelming sense of bereavement," he said to his son Christopher in a letter several months after Edith's passing. He was alone in the house for the first time in more than five decades. He continued in this letter, "Someone close in heart to me should know something about things that records do not record: the dreadful suffering of our childhoods, from which we rescued one another, but could not wholly heal the wounds . . . "

LITERARY CONNECTIONS

Edith Tolkien (née Bratt) has an entire book written about her. *The Gallant Edith Bratt* is a 286-page book written by Nancy Bunting and Seamus Hamil-Keays. It explores Edith's life from her birth in 1889 until the time she turned 28 in 1917. The descriptor "gallant" is a nod to how her husband once described her: "Edith [. . .] is very gallant."

The Tolkien Society

It should come as no surprise that Tolkien's love for clubs spilled over to his audience. Founded in 1969, The Tolkien Society is an international fan club as well as a literary society and charity organization dedicated to "promoting the life and works of the author and academic J.R.R. Tolkien." Tolkien himself agreed to be the honorary president of the society and indeed remains the president to this day. Upon his death, the society offered the role of honorary president to his son Christopher, but he declined the invitation. Christopher felt that his father should hold the title forever. Tolkien's daughter, Priscilla, served as the honorary vice president of the society and, just as with her father, is commemorated with holding that position even after her death.

The society encourages research and continued study of Tolkien's works, with specific emphasis on mythology, philology, and the fantasy genre. "Tolkien is the father of modern fantasy, whether people like that or not!" said Shaun Gunner, the chair of The Tolkien Society in an interview exclusively for this book. "My hope is the growing Middle-earth ecosystem will bring people to Tolkien." It was The Tolkien Society that created the annual March 25 event known as Tolkien Reading Day.

The society also publishes a bimonthly magazine called *Amon Hen* featuring articles, reviews, and reports relating to Tolkien's various works. There is also a significant social aspect to the club; members meet yearly at the gathering known as Oxonmoot, held at Oxford on the weekend closest to Bilbo's and Frodo's birthday (September 22).

THE MORE YOU KNOW

Ever the devoted fans of Tolkien's work, The Tolkien Society published a congratulatory birthday message in *The Times* for his eightieth birthday in 1972. They also sent him a gift of tobacco, along with the note: "FROM all Hobbits, Elves, Elf-friends, Dwarves, Ents, Numenoreans, Rohirrim, etc. etc. etc. of the TOLKIEN SOCIETY (in Britain) with love and honour and hearty congratulations, to the creator of so much wonder. Although not to be compared with the true LONGBOTTOM LEAF, we hope that this will at least raise a few smoke-rings of happy recollection."

Zimmerman & Boorman

Adapting a book into a movie is a tricky thing: Hundreds of pages of dialogue, description, and internal thought processes have to be condensed into a visual medium, and some aspects always get lost. J.R.R. Tolkien famously did not like people adapting his works. His first experiences with adaptation did not go well. Writing to his son Christopher and daughter-in-law Faith in 1957, he describes a visit by an American film agent named Forrest J. Ackerman. Tolkien and his publishers made the terms for any Middle-earth film very clear: "*Art or Cash.* Either very profitable terms indeed; or absolute author's veto on objectionable features or alterations"

The chance at a first-ever Lord of the Rings film script was given to Morton Grady Zimmerman. But the screenplay never made it to the silver screen. Tolkien wasn't happy with changes Zimmerman made. One such change had an eagle named Radagast show up in the Shire. Another gave the humanoid orcs beaks and feathers. Tolkien was not pleased: "I feel very unhappy about the extreme silliness and incompetence of Z and his complete lack of respect for the original."

While Zimmerman's screenplay was the first, the John Boorman script is perhaps the most infamous. His 1970 screenplay of The Lord of the Rings is a somewhat more bizarre look at Professor Tolkien's work. Aside from attempting to adapt the entire trilogy into one three-hour film, the characters behave remarkably out of character. Arwen appears as a kind of spirit or ghost to point the fellowship in the right direction. Boromir kisses Galadriel "with a flush of passion," but she rejects him and kisses Frodo in the next scene. It's then alluded to that she and Frodo spent the night together. As one scene early in the script described, "Suddenly they are in a field of buttercups. Naked children run and play among the golden flowers. The HOBBITS blink and grin and MERRY belches."

Yet, according to a 2012 interview with Boorman, it wasn't the script that kept the film from making it to the silver screen but rather the budget. United Artists held the rights to the movie adaptation of The Lord of the Rings but had run out of money to fund the project. It was ultimately abandoned. Would-be director Boorman later said he was actually glad his adaptation didn't get made because "it would mean that Pete Jackson's fantastic trilogy would not have been made."

THE MORE YOU KNOW

John Boorman had the distinct honor of meeting J.R.R. Tolkien, who asked him if he intended the film to be animated or live action. Boorman noted in a 1981 issue of the *Winnipeg Free Press* that Tolkien had been pleased to learn that the film would not be animated.

"Bilbo's Last Song" & Tolkien's Death

The final piece of literature J.R.R. Tolkien ever wrote in his life almost never saw the light of day. Tolkien fans have Margaret Joy Hill to thank for "Bilbo's Last Song." In June 1968, Tolkien fell down a flight of stairs while preparing to move to a different home. Now seventy-six years old, Tolkien had injured his leg so badly that it required surgery and a cast. It also "proved disastrous for my work and arrangements at this time." Realizing he would not be able to work as previously, he hired a secretary, Margaret Joy Hill. Amid the numerous daily tasks she completed to help The Professor in his later years, Hill found the poem "Bilbo's Last Song" while shelving books in his library.

As she described, "Something dropped out from between two of them. It was an exercise book: just the cover with a single sheet between, and on the page, a poem. [Tolkien] asked what it was; I gave it to him, and he read it aloud. It was Bilbo's Last Song." As a thank-you gift, Tolkien gave Hill the ownership of the copyright of the poem to do with as she wanted.

It was a fitting final gesture by the author. On September 2, 1973, John Ronald Reuel Tolkien passed away at the age of eighty-one in Bournemouth, England. He is buried in Wolvercote Cemetery in Oxford next to his wife, Edith.

Literary Connections

The year of Tolkien's death contains the same number of rings (though out of order) made or given to the peoples of Middle-earth: nine for men, seven for dwarves, and three for elves, with one ring to rule them all.

From "Bilbo's Last Song"

Day is ended, dim my eyes,
but journey long before me lies.
Farewell, friends! I hear the call.
The Ship's beside the stony wall.

. . .

Guided by the Lonely Star,
beyond the utmost harbour-bar
I'll find the havens fair and free,
and beaches of the Starlit Sea.
Ship, my ship! I seek the West,
and fields and mountains ever blest.
Farewell to Middle-Earth at last.
I see the Star above your mast!

Christopher Tolkien

It is difficult to know just how much of J.R.R. Tolkien's continued legacy is owed to his son, Christopher. The youngest son of John's four children, Christopher was involved in his father's work for most of his life. In fact, his involvement in Middle-earth started as early as age four or five, when he corrected his father on several inaccuracies in *The Hobbit*. In the foreword to the fiftieth anniversary edition of the book, Christopher recounts telling his father: "'Last time, you said Bilbo's front door was blue, and you said Thorin had a gold tassel on his hood, but you've just said that Bilbo's front door was green, and the tassel on Thorin's hood was silver'; at which point my father muttered 'Damn the boy,' and then 'strode across the room' to his desk to make a note."

After his father's passing in 1973, Christopher (then forty-nine years old) acted as the literary executor of the Tolkien estate for many years. J.R.R. Tolkien gave Christopher two options in his will: The first granted him full power to "publish, edit, alter, rewrite, or complete any work of mine which may be unpublished at my death." The second gave him the ability to "destroy the whole or any part or parts of any such unpublished works as he in his absolute discretion may think fit." Fortunately for Tolkien fans and scholars across the globe, Christopher chose to publish his father's works, and followed his father's instructions to the letter.

Described by many as a perfectionist and never satisfied with what he wrote, the elder Tolkien is famous for keeping all his notes on Middle-earth's history (even if the more recent writings contradicted older writings). He is also famous for writing over old notes with new ones. After his father's death, Christopher began compiling these notes and constructing the story that was his father's unpublished magnum opus, *The Silmarillion.* He would spend the rest of his life (forty-seven more years, to be precise) organizing his father's notes into a twelve-volume series called The History of Middle-earth. (More on these works later!) In 2016, Christopher was awarded a Bodley Medal, recognizing his outstanding contributions to literature.

LITERARY CONNECTIONS

Ever devoted to his father's work, Christopher was very critical of Peter Jackson's film trilogy. He considered the films to be more like action movies, lacking the depth of the books. Despite the length and scope of the films compared to previous adaptations, Christopher did not consider them to be a faithful adaptation of his father's work.

Dungeons & Dragons and Legal Action

Published first in 1974, *Dungeons & Dragons* is a tabletop role-playing game (often shortened to TTRPG). Armed with a few books, a pen and paper, as well as their powers of imagination, a group of people gather around a table or online meeting to play a game that takes place in their collective imagination. (Players can also use miniature versions of their characters and the enemy combatants, and even create maps for the dungeons.)

The first part of this lawsuit centered around a TTRPG created in the mid-1970s by a man named Larry Smith, who called his game The Battle of Five Armies. Lifted directly from Tolkien's battle in *The Hobbit,* the game pits the armies of elves, men, and dwarves against an army of orcs and wargs. Gary Gygax and Don Kaye, then owners of TSR Hobbies, purchased the rights to the game, and when the game's second edition came out under TSR, they kept some of the names Smith used—names that had been created and trademarked by Tolkien and used in The Lord of the Rings and *The Hobbit.* Gygax himself wrote on the *EN World* online forum in 2003 that Smith's attorney claimed the work was grandfathered in because of lapsed publishing rights and before any renewals were made.

Regardless, the cease-and-desist letter that followed would haunt the *DnD* legacy—and still does. The Tolkien Estate took issue with these words used in the game: "dragon," "dwarf," "elf," "ent," "goblin," "hobbit," "orc," "balrog," and "warg." Lawyers argued that all but three of these words had been used often enough throughout history that they were now part of the public domain; in the end, TSR changed the hobbits to halflings, the ents to treants, and the fearsome balrogs to balors.

THE MORE YOU KNOW

It has been established by *Dungeons & Dragons* lore that balors do in fact have wings. As to whether the balrogs of Middle-earth have actual wings or the ability to fly continues to be a topic of mostly humorous debate within the Tolkien community.

The Silmarillion

While The Lord of the Rings trilogy and *The Hobbit* tell the tale of the Third Age of Middle-earth, *The Silmarillion* tells the tale of almost everything else in J.R.R. Tolkien's legendarium. From the creation of the universe by the god Eru Ilúvatar, to the Atlantis-like utopia of Númenor where Aragorn's ancestors lived alongside dancing bears, Tolkien described *The Silmarillion* as "the history of the War of the Exiled Elves against the Enemy, which all takes place in the North-west of the world (Middle-earth)."

As mentioned previously, the origins of Middle-earth began for Tolkien around 1914 in Oxford, where he was a student. Tales of Middle-earth stayed with him in the trenches of France, and remained present in his mind through his years as an Oxford professor. But *The Silmarillion* never reached bookshelves during Tolkien's lifetime. It wouldn't be published until 1977, a few years after his death.

The More You Know

Before it was *The Silmarillion,* Tolkien called the story of the First and Second Ages of Middle-earth *The Book of Lost Tales.* The tales make up a grand and sweeping mythology of the world containing Middle-earth known as Eä.

The Silmarillion is made up of five parts. First is *Ainulindalë*, which bears similarities to the creation story found in the Catholic Bible. The god Eru Ilúvatar creates powerful beings known as Ainur, who, through music, create the physical world. The second part, *Valaquenta*, describes these powerful beings. The third part, *Quenta Silmarillion*, which takes up most of the pages in *The Silmarillion*, chronicles the events of the time before and during the First Age, and the almost five-hundred-year-long war between the elves and Melkor after he steals three sacred jewels from the elves known as the Silmarils. The fourth part, *Akallabêth*, takes readers through the events of the Second Age, chronicling the history and downfall of the island of Númenor. As explored earlier in this book, Númenor was Tolkien's version of Atlantis. The fifth and final portion of the book is a brief recap of the events of *The Hobbit* and The Lord of the Rings.

After Tolkien's death in 1973, his son Christopher, alongside fantasy writer Guy Gavriel Kay, spent the next four years compiling all the notes that make up these five parts into a cohesive story. While it didn't have the same kind of adventure and whimsy as *The Hobbit* or The Lord of the Rings, it finally arrived on bookshelves, just as The Professor had hoped for his entire life.

From The Silmarillion

Those of the Elven-race that lived still in Middle-earth waned and faded, and Men usurped the sunlight. Then the Quendi wandered in the lonely places of the great lands and the isles, and took to the moonlight and the starlight, and to the woods and caves, becoming as shadows and memories, save those who ever and anon set sail into the West and vanished from Middle-earth.

The Great Tales

Found within *The Silmarillion* are three tales that recount the most important events of the First Age: *Beren and Lúthien*, *The Children of Húrin*, and *The Fall of Gondolin.* Known as the Great Tales, these three stories got their start back in the 1910s while Tolkien was still in school. Within *The Silmarillion*, Christopher Tolkien condensed and structured the tales so they are told within the context of the larger story. Many of the more obscure details were omitted.

Tolkien's books grew so much in popularity that eventually stand-alone books were published of all three tales, with details Tolkien had included added back in. These books gave readers significantly more details to delve into about Middle-earth, as well as a unique glimpse into the creative process Tolkien used to construct the major events of his legendarium. Christopher provides a running commentary alongside each version of the story told in the various drafts printed in these books.

An atmosphere of fate and doom hangs over all three tales. Published as a stand-alone book in April 2007, *The Children of Húrin* seems to be Tolkien's attempt at Greek tragedy. Explored more later in this book, *The Children of Húrin* is filled with misfortune, betrayal, and tragic death.

Beren and Lúthien was published separately nearly a decade later, in 2017. As discussed previously, this tale follows a human, Beren, and an elf, Lúthien, who fall in love and must risk their lives to complete the quest that will allow them to be together. Also discussed previously, *The Fall of Gondolin* was published as an individual book one year after *Beren and Lúthien*, in August 2018. It tells the tale of a secret elven city and its ultimate destruction at the hands of evil made possible by a great betrayal. Each of these stories features tragic heroes and adds to the foundation previously established in The Lord of the Rings.

Literary Connections

The origin of the mythical island of Atlantis that Tolkien used to create the island of Númenor came from Greek philosopher Plato. This myth tells the tale of a powerful and technologically advanced island nation founded by the god Poseidon somewhere near the modern-day Strait of Gibraltar. Most scholars believe Plato created the story as a political and moral argument about ideal states and ethics as well as the fall of civilizations.

The Children of Húrin

The Children of Húrin is about as close to a Greek tragedy as Tolkien gets in his legendarium. Originally published as Chapter 21 in *The Silmarillion*, the tale follows the tragic life of a man named Túrin in the First Age of Middle-earth. Túrin's father, Húrin, is captured by the dark lord Morgoth, and his whole family is cursed. Meanwhile, Húrin, "the man who had dared to defy and to scorn him [Morgoth] to his face" is bound to a chair and forced to watch the fate of his family play out over decades.

What follows is a tale that many consider to be one of Tolkien's most devastating; Húrin's daughter Niënor is bewitched by the dragon Glaurung and unwittingly falls in love with her own brother, Túrin. Túrin, in the midst of his adventures, kills a dear friend, unknowingly marries his own sister, and fathers a child with her. It is only after these events unfold and all is revealed do the main characters feel the full impact of the twisted curse that befell his family.

Tolkien's views on fate in this story combine with a tragic irony that parallels Greek tales like Oedipus Rex and Norse myths like the *Saga of the Völsungs*. It is considered by many to be one of Tolkien's darkest stories by far, emphasizing the nature of evil and corruption. Tolkien also drew inspiration for this tragic tale from the epic poem *Kalevala*. Within this poem is "The Story of Kullervo," which follows a man whose family is slaughtered or enslaved by the evil Untamo. Turin's own story arc follows a similar pattern to Kullervo's. Tolkien had written to his future wife, Edith Bratt, in October 1914: "Amongst other work I am trying to turn one of the stories – which is really a very great story and most tragic – into a short story. . . . " The story was "The Story of Kullervo." Tolkien had translated and retold this story as an undergraduate at Exeter College in 1914.

LITERARY CONNECTIONS

Kalevala **was created by a man named Elias Lönnrot. Lönnrot, born in Finland, took the myths, folk tales, and heroic poems of Finnish origin and compiled them into one interconnected tale. The type of tale Lönnrot created is what's known as a mythic cycle. It encapsulates a mythical universe, and typically does not follow the traditional beginning, middle, and end style of storytelling. Instead, it created a mythological universe where many stories unfold.**

Rankin/Bass

Arthur Rankin Jr. and Jules Bass are responsible for two feature films set in Middle-earth. In 1977, Rankin and Bass brought Middle-earth to life in the same way Tolkien himself did: with drawings. But these drawings moved and could be watched on television. With a budget of $3 million (roughly $16 million today adjusted for inflation), the first feature was a made-for-TV movie of *The Hobbit*.

This movie had a mixed reception. It won the Peabody Award, an award for distinguished achievement and merit in broadcast and digital media, and a Christopher Award, given to creators of works that "affirm the highest values of the human spirit." It was also nominated for a Hugo Award, an award honoring fantasy and science fiction works. On the opposite end of the spectrum, the movie was criticized for uneven animation and for omitting key plot points like the Arkenstone and Beorn the skin-changer. *The New York Times* reviewer John J. O'Connor called it "curiously eclectic," while science fiction author Baird Searles called it an "abomination."

Rankin and Bass returned three years later, in 1980, with their animated adaptation of *The Return of the King*. The film begins after Frodo Baggins and Samwise Gamgee have already entered Mordor. Though the plots of *The Fellowship of the Ring* and *The Two Towers* are not dramatized (but rather narrated in voiceover by Gandalf), several voice actors from *The Hobbit* film returned for their roles in this film. It features a number of original songs that have become cult classics, including "Where There's a Whip, There's a Way" and "Frodo of the Nine Fingers."

The film was once again criticized for the uneven animation and oversimplification of an incredibly complicated plot. "We tried to do *Return of the King*," said Arthur Rankin Jr. in an interview at the Museum of Television and Radio in 2003. "But it is an awful lot to put into it . . . it's not a very good film."

THE MORE YOU KNOW

The studio that created the animation for *The Hobbit* and *The Return of the King* was called Topcraft. The studio had already worked with Rankin and Bass for several holiday stories, including *Frosty's Winter Wonderland* in 1976. Beyond that, they had a hand in several adaptations including of *The Wizard of Oz*, *The Last Unicorn*, and *ThunderCats*. Financial hardship would force Topcraft to declare bankruptcy in 1985. It was then that legendary animator Hayao Miyazaki, as well as several other animators from Topcraft, formed Studio Ghibli. Four of Studio Ghibli's films currently reside on the list of the top-ten highest-grossing Japanese feature films.

Ralph Bakshi

In between the release of the animated version of *The Hobbit* and the animated version of *The Return of the King*, another animated film was made that bridges that gap of the Middle-earth story. Released in 1978, Ralph Bakshi's *Lord of the Rings* was told with technology that some believe fell short of making Tolkien a commercial success at the box office. As documentarian Dan Olson remarked in his video *An Exhaustive History of Ralph Bakshi's Lord of the Rings*, "In a weird way, Bakshi's *Lord of the Rings* is a twenty-first century blockbuster made with twentieth-century technology." The animation style is a unique combination of rotoscoping (painting over live-action actors), solarization (black-and-white film developed twice), and several other techniques. In a 1978 interview, Bakshi himself referred to the film as "the first realistic painting in motion picture." The cast has a few notable names, including John Hurt as Aragorn and Anthony Daniels (C-3PO from Star Wars) as Legolas.

Some of the film's stylistic choices drew criticism at the time. For instance, Boromir wears a stereotypical two-horned Viking helmet. Also, during portions of the film, including the battle between Gandalf and the balrog, the live-action actors mostly become visible. Additionally, the movie tells a largely unfinished story, ending after the events of the Battle of Helm's Deep due to budget constraints. Bakshi's *Lord of the Rings* was and continues to be divisive among viewers, and responses to the film have spanned a wide range.

Despite the setbacks, mixed reception, and unfinished narrative, Bakshi's film set a new standard in filmmaking. As Dan Olson remarked in his documentary video, the idea of combining live action and animation had been done before, but never on this scale: "The modern look of film is defined by actors on set wearing some combination of costume that's limiting of suggesting of the final look before artists go in afterwards and paint the rest of the costume on. . . . They saw what was inevitable about the way these technologies would be applied and bit off far more than they could chew decades before the tech was actually ready. . . . Once the odd fixation of a few weirdos from Brooklyn, is now the ordinary."

The More You Know

What started as a $3 million budget for Ralph Bakshi's *Lord of the Rings* ballooned to up to $12 million (roughly $60 million today when adjusted for inflation).

Unfinished Tales of Númenor and Middle-earth

Edited by Christopher Tolkien and published in 1980, J.R.R. Tolkien's *Unfinished Tales of Númenor and Middle-earth* contains stories that, as indicated by its very name, are incomplete. Different versions of different stories throughout Middle-earth's history can be found within the pages of this collection, including *The Children of Húrin*, one of the Great Tales mentioned previously in this book. There is no narrative cohesion in *Unfinished Tales* as there is in *The Silmarillion*. One story does not lead into the next. Instead, narrative fragments are presented in more detail. These add depth and complexity to a host of Middle-earth's most notorious characters, like Isildur, Túrin Turambar, and Galadriel.

Arranged in four parts, *Unfinished Tales of Númenor and Middle-earth* delves into the major stories of the First, Second, and Third Ages, as well as detailed accounts of some of the lesser-known aspects of Tolkien's fictional world like the Drúedain (wild men), the Istari (wizards), and the palantíri (seeing stones). The book also describes the arrival of Gandalf and the other Istari to Middle-earth, as well as a retelling of *The Hobbit* from Gandalf's perspective, titled "The Quest for Erebor."

Literary Connections

Peter Jackson drew inspiration from the *Unfinished Tales* story of "The Quest for Erebor" as he worked to bring *The Hobbit* to life on screen. He drew on the story to not only enrich The Hobbit film trilogy but also to connect the actions in that work to the eventual plot of The Lord of the Rings films.

The book sold well and ignited a desire in fans to know more about Middle-earth. Tolkien discussed this phenomenon before his passing, in a letter to his publisher: "It is, I suppose, a tribute to the curious effect that story has, when based on very elaborate and detailed workings of geography, chronology, and language, that so many should clamour for sheer 'information,' or 'lore.'"

Given the success of *Unfinished Tales*, it was clear that there was still great interest in Tolkien's work. This would pave the way for Christopher's own magnum opus: a twelve-volume series called The History of Middle-earth.

From Unfinished Tales of Númenor and Middle-earth ("The Disaster of the Gladden Fields")

The Orcs were now drawing near. Isildur turned to his esquire: "Ohtar," he said, "I give this now to your keeping"; and he delivered to him the great sheath and the shards of Narsil, Elendil's sword. "Save it from capture by all means that you can find and at all costs; even at the cost of being held a coward who deserted me."

The History of Middle-earth

By 1981, Christopher Tolkien had nearly 2,000 pages worth of notes written by his father over his lifetime. But what to do with them all? "You will perceive," Christopher explained in a letter to the publisher, "that it is in no conceivable way publishable." What followed was the intense and laborious process of making the unpublishable publishable.

Christopher had spent the previous decade since his father's passing organizing Tolkien's notes into a cohesive narrative, and published both *The Silmarillion* and *Unfinished Tales of Númenor and Middle-earth*. The demand for those books among Tolkien's avid readers set the stage for Christopher's twelve-volume series called The History of Middle-earth, which aimed to tell not just the stories of Middle-earth but also the development of Tolkien's imagination and intentions as he crafted his fantastical universe. It would take Christopher and the team at Allen & Unwin another thirteen years to finish all twelve volumes.

The sheer disorganization of his father's notes made them difficult to parse through. Christopher often found notes about characters on the margins of pages of other works or on piles of papers that contradicted each other. Not to mention the hundreds of letters written by Tolkien that provided the minutia about the world of Middle-earth that readers love so much. Christopher also had the monumental task of extrapolating from where his father's notes ended to provide his own commentary.

Featuring completely new material as well as earlier versions of stories previously published, the volumes were released at a rate of about one per year, beginning in 1983 and ending in 1996. The first two volumes—*The Book of Lost Tales: Part One*, published in 1983, and *The Book of Lost Tales: Part Two*, published in 1984—can often be found together at bookstores. These first two volumes laid the groundwork for how the full History of Middle-earth would take shape. Each would include many of Tolkien's tales, like the origin of the sun and the moon or the fall of Gondolin, told in as much detail as was available.

The critical response to this massive series was and continues to be varied. For some readers, it is a slow and often laborious undertaking. "I'll admit I screeched to a halt on Vol. 3—an entire book of poetry is a bit much for me," said one reader. In Tolkien forums, others noted that they made it a point to read each book that came out as soon as it was published. It wasn't just Tolkien's world they wanted to know more about; it was also his mind.

As Tolkien scholar Charles Noad wrote in a 1994 article in *Mallorn: The Journal of the Tolkien Society*, "It reveals far more about Tolkien's invented world than any of his readers in pre-*Silmarillion* days could ever have imagined or hoped for."

LITERARY CONNECTIONS

C.S. Lewis contributed to shaping *The Lay of Leithian,* the long poem making up the third part of *The Lays of Beleriand,* the third book in The History of Middle-earth. After first reading the material, Lewis said, "I can quite honestly say that it is ages since I have had an evening of such delight: and the personal interest of reading a friend's work had very little to do with it." Lewis went on to write a critique of the work, and Tolkien made several minor changes based on Lewis's notes.

Within the long list of adaptations of Middle-earth are two infamous creations, both produced in Russia. The first was a miniseries of The Lord of the Rings called *Хранители*, or *Khraniteli*, which roughly translates to *Guardians* or *Keepers* (i.e., of the One Ring). Much like the One Ring itself, this adaptation had its moment of power and then went dormant, waiting to be rediscovered (though for only thirty years instead of three thousand).

Directed by Natalya Serebryakova, *Khraniteli* is a low-budget production by Leningrad Television that aired only once on TV, in 1991 (after which, it was thought to be lost). The Soviet Union would collapse later that year, and with it vanished this bizarre yet whimsical adaptation. . . . That is, until someone at Leningrad Television's successor, Channel 5, rediscovered the miniseries three decades later, in 2021, and posted it on YouTube. With a 115-minute run time split between two parts, it includes a number of scenes not found in many other adaptations of Tolkien. Both Tom Bombadil and his wife, Goldberry, make an appearance, as do the barrow-wights that haunt the hobbits throughout their misadventure in the Old Forest. As another unique aspect of this adaptation, the character of Legolas was played by the director's daughter!

The reaction to the re-release of the miniseries on YouTube led to a cult following. Viewers found it funny (even hilariously horrifying). Just a few days after it was uploaded to the streaming platform, Part 1 reached over half a million views.

The More You Know

Lesser known than *Khraniteli* is a 1985 Soviet-era adaptation of *The Hobbit* known as *The Fabulous Journey of Mr. Bilbo Baggins, the Hobbit, Across the Wild Land, Through the Dark Forest, Beyond the Misty Mountains. There and Back Again.* It is a little more than an hour long, and does not feature either the elves of Rivendell, the trolls, or the skin-changer Beorn.

The Last Ringbearer

The 1999 book *The Last Ringbearer* is the second infamous adaptation of the tales of Middle-earth to come from Russia . . . and is often considered one of the more controversial. In this reinterpretation of The Lord of the Rings, Russian paleontologist and author Kirill Yeskov took a significantly more realistic approach to the political dealings of Middle-earth. The book has become a cult classic, despite never having been officially published outside Russia.

The Last Ringbearer takes place at the very end of the third book in the trilogy, *The Return of the King*. In this version of the story, the armies of Mordor and their allies have been soundly defeated, and the One Ring is destroyed; it seems evil is defeated. Yet Yeskov portrays the culture of Mordor very differently. The so-called dark magic used by Sauron is scientific advancement and technological prowess. The elves Galadriel and Elrond (alongside the wizard Gandalf) are political elitists and warmongers seeking to sway the common folk to their side. The book does not directly address real-world politics, but some believe that it is a criticism of American exceptionalism.

Not every fan of The Professor's work who has read this book responds to it fondly. It was widely panned by most critics, and scholars have referred to as both a parody and a paraquel (a story that takes place at the same time from a different perspective). Despite being very popular among Russian Tolkien fans and translated into English in 2010, it has never had an official translation, most likely due to copyright concerns with the Tolkien Estate: "Translations of the book have also appeared in other European nations, but fear of the vigilant and litigious Tolkien estate has heretofore prevented its publication in English," according to journalist Laura Miller, writing in *Salon*.

LITERARY CONNECTIONS

Of the many translations of The Lord of the Rings, the Swedish version published in 2005 is widely regarded as one of the most successful. For accuracy and authenticity, *Ringarnas herre*, translated by Erik Andersson and Lotta Olsson, incorporates Old Norse words, which blends well with Tolkien's writing style, as he incorporated many Old Norse words in his texts.

Peter Jackson

While book and low-budget film adaptations were developing a cult following across Russia, New Zealand director Peter Jackson was pitching a two-film live-action adaptation of The Lord of the Rings trilogy to various film production companies. Fresh off of the success of his film *Heavenly Creatures*, Jackson was a lifelong fan of Tolkien's work. Several of the production companies he approached, including Miramax, passed on the rights to adapt Tolkien's books, until Jackson's WingNut Films eventually got the rights through New Line Cinema. But the deal with New Line Cinema was for three films, not two. So, the work began.

Over the course of the next five years, the films (which were all shot simultaneously between October 1999 and December 2000) were made with painstaking detail. Entire sets were built in quarries, and the gorgeous landscape of New Zealand was utilized to capture the look of Middle-earth. The production budget totaled $281 million (equivalent to $530 million in 2025!).

The films proved to be a commercial and cultural success, grossing nearly $3 billion worldwide. Written by Jackson alongside his partner, Fran Walsh, and his friend Philippa Boyens, The Lord of the Rings would be nominated for eight hundred different awards and wind up winning 475 of them. The wins included seventeen of their thirty Academy Awards nominations, and thirteen of their thirty-five British Academy Film Award (BAFTA) nominations.

Peter Jackson's connections to Tolkien and The Lord of the Rings did not stop with this trilogy, however. He went on to serve as executive producer on The Hobbit trilogy, released from 2012 to 2014. Originally meant to be two films directed by Guillermo del Toro, Jackson stepped in to direct the films after del Toro's departure. Martin Freeman's casting as Bilbo Baggins and Sir Ian McKellen's and Orlando Bloom's returning roles as Gandalf and Legolas, respectively, likely helped propel the film to box office success, each film grossing around $1 billion.

In May 2024, it was announced that Jackson would be co-producing another film in Tolkien's universe—this one focused on Gollum. Andy Serkis, who plays Gollum in The Lord of the Rings, would reprise his role and act as director.

THE MORE YOU KNOW

During the Battle of Helm's Deep in *The Two Towers*, the Uruk-hai war cry that strikes fear in viewers was actually a sound bite that Peter Jackson generated at a New Zealand cricket match. Jackson went onto the pitch between innings and led the fans in growling and shouting from the stands. He later edited these sounds into the background during the epic battle scenes.

Christopher Lee & Ian Holm

One of the crucial elements that made Peter Jackson's *Lord of the Rings* trilogy so successful was the cast. Actors like Elijah Wood, Miranda Otto, Orlando Bloom, and Cate Blanchett would become synonymous with their Middle-earth characters. It bears mention that while J.R.R. Tolkien's life was quite full, it perhaps pales in comparison to that of the actor who plays Saruman.

Sir Christopher Frank Carandini Lee was known as a powerhouse of pop culture during his lifetime. After volunteering for and subsequently being grounded from the Royal Air Force during World War II, Lee began working as an intelligence officer. His military service went on to inspire his step-cousin, author Ian Fleming, to create one of the most iconic fictional secret agents ever, James Bond. After his time in the military, Lee would go on to become a successful actor, appearing in 266 films during his lifetime. "Christopher, I think, wrote to Tolkien so many times," said co-star John Rhys-Davies. "It was one of his great dreams to play Gandalf. And I think he may have actually had Tolkien's blessing to do that. He is such a remarkable actor."

Christopher Lee did in fact meet J.R.R. Tolkien. "It was in a pub that he used to go to in Oxford, called the Eagle and

Child," recounted Lee in a 2003 interview. "I was there having a beer and I was completely overcome when he walked in. I had already started reading the books and thought, 'This man has created a unique form of literature—one of the great works of all time.' . . . I'm still an enormous fan—I read The Lord of the Rings every year."

Alongside Lee, actor Sir Ian Holm also has a profound connection to The Professor's legacy, one that spans thirty years. Despite appearing in at least seventy-two films and over thirty television shows, Ian Holm is perhaps best known for playing the role of Bilbo Baggins in *The Fellowship of the Ring* and *The Return of the King*. But before he got the role of Bilbo, Holm played Bilbo's much younger cousin, Frodo Baggins, in the BBC Radio 4 adaptation of The Lord of the Rings. Holm would also reprise his Bilbo role for two of the three films of The Hobbit trilogy.

THE MORE YOU KNOW

A talented singer, Christopher Lee added his voice to the Danish musical group the Tolkien Ensemble. Lee's booming voice fit the role of Treebeard. He also provided narration for two of the group's four albums, whose covers feature the original illustrations by Queen Margrethe II of Denmark for The Lord of the Rings. The Tolkien Ensemble formed in 1995 to create "the world's first complete musical interpretation of the poems and songs from The Lord of the Rings."

From The Fellowship of the Ring

"I wish it need not have happened in my time," said Frodo.

"So do I," said Gandalf, "and so do all who live to see such times. But that is not for them to decide. All we have to decide is what to do with the time that is given to us."

They Shall Not Grow Old

After his team's adaptation of The Lord of the Rings trilogy won seventeen Academy Awards, Peter Jackson went on to produce and direct two historical documentaries, including one called *They Shall Not Grow Old.* Commissioned by the Imperial War Museum (IWM) and the BBC, Jackson combed through over six hundred hours of black-and-white footage of World War I for this technicolor high-definition documentary about the war that so greatly impacted Tolkien's own life and writing.

"I wanted to reach through the fog of time and pull these men into the modern world, so they can regain their humanity once more—rather than be seen only as Charlie Chaplin–type figures in the vintage archive film," Jackson said.

Released in 2018, *They Shall Not Grow Old* used state-of-the-art technology at the time to restore color and improve the frame rate of actual film from World War I—35-millimeter film that was more than one hundred years old. Some fans consider this movie to be very close to what J.R.R. Tolkien experienced during his time fighting in World War I, from the propaganda used to recruit soldiers like him, to their enlistment and training, to their life in the trenches and in combat. Fans of his work can watch this film to dig deeper into what it was like to be a young soldier in the Great War. Rather than using voice-over by historians to narrate the footage as is usually done in documentaries, the movie relies on real interviews of World War I soldiers recorded by the BBC and the IWM. *They Shall Not Grow Old* was nominated for a BAFTA, and served as a kind of springboard for Jackson's other documentary project: *The Beatles: Get Back*. Jackson and his team used the same techniques to make that film, which was released in 2021.

THE MORE YOU KNOW

In an interview about his work on *The Beatles: Get Back*, Peter Jackson discussed the Beatles' Lord of the Rings film that never came to be. Paul McCartney told Jackson that he was glad they never got to do the film because that left the door open for the Jackson trilogy. Jackson, a huge Beatles fan, said it was a shame that the Beatles missed out—in his mind, it would have been an incredible musical adaptation of Tolkien's series.

Tolkien-Related Holidays

Many unofficial holidays have come from popular franchises. May the Fourth (which comes from the quote "May the Force be with you") acts as a day of celebration for Star Wars fans across the globe. In the Tolkien community, fans have opted to not use calendar puns for their celebration; instead, they have picked a specific date that honors the Father of Modern Fantasy.

Tolkien Reading Day is March 25. This is the same day (in the year 3019 of the Third Age of Middle-earth) that the hobbits Frodo and Sam complete the quest to destroy the One Ring. The holiday first came about in 2002 when Sean Kirst, a columnist for a local Syracuse, New York, paper, wrote to The Tolkien Society, asking: "[I]s there any day devoted informally to reading from the trilogy?" The committee that oversees The Tolkien Society loved the inquiry so much that they made March 25, 2003, the first-ever Tolkien Reading Day.

Every year on March 25, you'll find members of the Tolkien community engaged in any number of events to honor The Professor's memory. On social media, people share their favorite passages from Tolkien's works. Some communities host live in-person readings with friends or online live streams with guest readers. Others use this day to start book clubs.

But what about a second Tolkien-related holiday? Falling on Bilbo and Frodo's mutual birthday, September 22 is widely recognized among Tolkien fans as Hobbit Day. This holiday invites readers and fans of Middle-earth to channel their inner hobbit for twenty-four hours. A walk by a local park might offer the sight of families and friends gathered for a massive picnic where some (if not most) attendees are dressed in hobbit-related attire. Movie marathons of either of Peter Jackson's trilogies might be hosted, accompanied by a multicourse meal that spans the entire day. Many Renaissance fairs will also host special events for Hobbit Day, like the Elevenses Toast and the Hobbit Dance Party. As the American Tolkien Society describes the holiday, "This is perhaps the oldest festal observance associated with Tolkien fandom. Celebration actually predates the formal designation of the holiday." The American Tolkien Society first made mention of a Hobbit Day in 1978.

LITERARY CONNECTIONS

J.R.R. Tolkien's hobbits originated as a wandering folk who observed a calendar that was guided by the moon, with the new year beginning after the harvest. Shortly after coming into contact with people outside their nomadic groups, they eventually adopted a different system, taking on the notion of weeks in addition to months. This is referred to as the Shire-reckoning.

Sing Me a Tale of the Greatest of Them All

Despite the fact that The Lord of the Rings contains more than sixty poems and songs, it took more than fifty years to turn the series into a musical. *The Lord of the Rings* had its first run in 2006 in Toronto, Canada. The adaptation was quite the heavy lift for the production team—so much so that significant changes were required.

The musical boasted a three-and-a-half-hour-long run time, about an hour of which was music. One of the composers, A.R. Rahman, wrote the Academy Award–winning score for 2008's Best Picture winner, *Slumdog Millionaire.* Matthew Warchus took the lead as director of the sixty-five different actors cast in the production.

Split into three acts, this production had the monumental task of turning a trilogy of books into a musical that could be enjoyed in one sitting. While the musical holds fairly true to events in the book, major cuts were made, so that most of the story arc of *The Two Towers* takes about thirty minutes. The reception to the first run was mixed. Some of the musical numbers and the set and costume design received praise. Meanwhile, Ben Brantley of *The*

New York Times called it "incomprehensible," while *The Daily Telegraph*'s Marianka Swain called it "disastrous." The show closed after less than six months.

A second production, in London in 2007, went through significant changes. Some songs and scenes were cut to reduce the run time to three hours. Reception to this production was more positive. Reviewer Michael Billington of *The Guardian* called it a "hugely impressive production." Renowned actress Dame Judy Dench called it a "terrific treat." The production had a thirteen-month run. A scaled-down version titled *The Lord of the Rings: A Musical Tale* was performed in Newbury, West Berkshire, England, in 2023; in Chicago and in Auckland, New Zealand, in 2024; and in Australia in 2025.

The More You Know

Creating *The Lord of the Rings* musical was an extremely expensive endeavor. The show in Toronto cost $26.9 million (equivalent to about $42 million today). The London show did not fare better, with a roughly $49 million price tag (equivalent to roughly $75 million today), earning it the dubious honor of being one of the costliest musical productions outside Las Vegas.

The Lord of the Rings Online

The rise of the Internet has led to interactive adaptations of Middle-earth lore. Just as so many readers have longed to escape to Middle-earth in their imagination, so, too, have some fans tried to escape to Tolkien's universe through the art of video games. Middle-earth-related video games first appeared in stores as early as 1982, with *The Hobbit* game. This was the first Tolkien-inspired 2D PC-style game available on a personal computer. However, the online game that's been going the longest—and is one of most beloved by fans—was released in April 2007.

The Lord of the Rings Online is a type of game known as a MMORPG, or a massively multiplayer online role-playing game. Players from across the world log on to their computers to role-play as characters of their own making within Middle-earth. It's like the award-winning *World of Warcraft* game but set in Middle-earth. Players choose to be an elf, a human, a dwarf, a hobbit, or even a skin-changer. Either traveling solo or joining up with friends and strangers, players then complete quests, explore dungeons, or take part in epic battles around Middle-earth.

The Lord of the Rings Online continues to be updated by Standing Stone Games as of 2025, eighteen years after its release. Through nearly two decades of gameplay, fans have been able to delve into the deep past of Middle-earth with this game. "The fact that it is Lord of the Rings carries so much weight," said LOTRO streamer Bludborn in an interview for this book: "The fandom is diehard. If given the opportunity and space to live in Middle-earth, they will."

The More You Know

Video games aren't the only way Lord of the Rings fans can immerse themselves in Tolkien's world. *The One Ring* (released in March 2022 by Free League Publishing) gives players the opportunity to experience Middle-earth in a tabletop format similar to that of *Dungeons & Dragons*, with players rolling six- and twelve-sided dice to resolve actions.

Tolkien Memes

Another fan-driven phenomenon found on the World Wide Web is Tolkien memes! First coined by author Richard Dawkins in his 1976 book *The Selfish Gene,* the word "meme" describes an idea or a behavior that spreads by means of imitation from person to person within a culture. Memes are typically images, videos, sounds, captions, or a combination of these. First becoming popular in the mid-to-late 2000s, memes have grown into one of the most circulated forms of media found online. They are most easily recognized by those in the community that the content is created for—and the Tolkien community has created a lot of memes.

Ian McKellen's now-famous delivery of the line "You shall not pass" has been referenced or repeated in hundreds of bits of media, including memes, since 2001 (though this line is actually changed from "You cannot pass," Tolkien's original text). Other popular Tolkien memes include an image of Sean Bean as Boromir during his "One does not simply walk into Mordor" monologue. It gained notoriety when fans discovered the reason Bean delivered that line so seriously while staring downward: He was reading his lines off the script in his lap!

In another meme, Dominic Monaghan, who plays Merry in The Lord of the Rings trilogy, uses a false accent to ask

Elijah Wood (who plays Frodo Baggins), "Do you wear wigs?" during an interview where Elijah couldn't see who was asking the question. All four of the actors who play the hobbits in the fellowship would take a group photo in 2023 in which they wore wigs—creating yet another meme. But perhaps the most iconic and well-known meme of Middle-earth concerns food. The question "What about second breakfast?" (posed by Pippin in *The Fellowship of the Ring*) has been asked or spoofed in every corner of the Internet in one variation or another. It was first made as a reference to the second breakfast Bilbo Baggins eats in *The Hobbit*.

Memes often have a very short shelf life, lasting anywhere from a day to a week. But some have more staying power, and even fewer withstand the test of time. It is a testament to the strength of the online community of Tolkien fans that a number of these enduring memes—even some created decades ago—relate to Middle-earth.

The More You Know

While The Lord of the Rings is under copyright until 2044, it is difficult to police the spread of memes on the Internet. Given the fair use argument, as long as the memes are not devaluing the original material, they can be justified as being used for education, parody, news reporting, or critical review.

The Rings of Power

The most recent live-action adaptation of Middle-earth is also the most expensive TV rights deal in history. In 2017, billionaire Jeff Bezos and the team at Amazon Prime Video purchased the rights to produce a Lord of the Rings television show. They did not get all the rights to Tolkien's works, however; they purchased only the rights to the appendices found in *The Return of the King*. Nevertheless, production began.

The Lord of the Rings: The Rings of Power focuses on characters featured in the Peter Jackson films, like Galadriel (played by Morfydd Clark) and Elrond (played by Robert Aramayo). Alongside them are characters who would appear only in the Second Age, like Durin IV (played by Owain Arthur) and Gil-galad (played by Benjamin Walker). Because of the limited rights, the show created new characters as well, including a few dozen hobbits (called Harfoots in the show) and several elves, dwarves, and humans. The show follows a condensed timeline of the events of the Second Age of Middle-earth, including Sauron's quest to dominate all life, and the heroes of Middle-earth who seek to stop him.

Released in 2022 and 2024, respectively, the first two seasons of the planned five for *The Rings of Power* have had a mixed reception. Many viewers have voiced their dislike for the show not sticking close enough to Tolkien's lore. Some call the plot of the first seasons somewhat disjointed. However, critics have praised the show for the music, cinematography, and acting.

THE MORE YOU KNOW

While Peter Jackson feels a sense of connection to The Lord of the Rings films, he was not directly involved in the production of *The Rings of Power*. He wasn't able to commit to a lengthy project because he was busy with the demands of producing and directing documentaries, and offered to serve in an advisory capacity instead. However, he noted in an interview that after being promised scripts to look at, Amazon did not reach out to him again.

From The Fellowship of the Ring ("Ring-verse")

Three Rings for the Elven-kings under the sky,
Seven for the Dwarf-lords in their halls of stone,
Nine for Mortal Men doomed to die,
One for the Dark Lord on his dark throne
In the Land of Mordor where the Shadows lie.
One Ring to rule them all, One Ring to find them,
One Ring to bring them all, and in the darkness
  bind them
In the Land of Mordor where the Shadows lie.

The War of the Rohirrim

In June 2021, in a nod to the twentieth anniversary of *The Lord of the Rings: The Fellowship of the Ring,* Warner Bros. announced the studio was developing a new animated Tolkien film. *The Lord of the Rings: The War of the Rohirrim* is also a return of sorts for the team that made Peter Jackson's film adaptations in the early 2000s.

The story of *The War of the Rohirrim* takes place more than 250 years before the events of the trilogy and follows the ninth king of Rohan. King Helm Hammerhand and his people are forced into a war with a neighboring tribe. Narrated by Miranda Otto, who plays Éowyn in the Peter Jackson films, the film is based on details in the appendices of The Lord of the Rings and focuses on King Helm Hammerhand's daughter. While she is unnamed in the appendices, this film names her Héra. Despite passing in 2015, Christopher Lee posthumously reprises his role as Saruman in this movie, through the use of archival recordings of the actor's voice.

THE MORE YOU KNOW

While Merry and Pippin do not appear in *The War of the Rohirrim,* actors Billy Boyd and Dominic Monaghan, who play the lovable hobbits in Jackson's trilogy, voice two orcs who capture Héra when she leaves the safety of Helm's Deep during a siege.

Tolkien Never Said That

Along with the popularity of online memes and forums come constant cycles of misinformation. Quotes are often attributed to people who never said anything of the sort, and J.R.R. Tolkien has not been an exception. On January 9, 2022, Elon Musk, the richest person in the world as of April 2025, posted an image to the social media website then known as Twitter. The image shows The Professor with his iconic suit jacket and pipe staring off camera at something. The text over the image reads: "The elites don't want you to know this but the ducks at the park are free. You can take them home. I have 458 ducks."

While some noted that it was ridiculous to even suggest that a single person (let alone a renowned author) could steal 458 ducks without getting caught, the rumor persisted. In forums all across the Internet, hundreds of people attributed the quote to Tolkien. However, the true origin of the quote is a user with the handle @weinerdog4life from May 3, 2018. The text (sometimes referred to as a copypasta) spread across dozens of websites, forums, and social media platforms in the intervening years.

And this is not the only misattribution to Tolkien! Another instance stems from the question asked by many critical readers of The Lord of the Rings: Why didn't the Fellowship of the Ring just take the eagles to Mordor? In April 2021, a forty-nine-second video was posted that some thought answered this question. In the video (which now has millions of views), a writer and voice actor named Asher Puls impersonates Tolkien to explain why: "I get this same question from people who run into me at the pub. . . . It would have made the quest a whole lot easier. And I tell them the same thing I'm telling you right now. . . . Shut up." Tolkien fans across the Internet attempted to decipher whether the voice in the video was actually The Professor's. In the end, Asher Puls put out a video explaining that the video in question features his voice and not Tolkien's.

THE MORE YOU KNOW

Tolkien included a painting of an eagle in some editions of *The Hobbit* that he painted himself. He drew inspiration from a painting of a golden eagle by Archibald Thorburn. This does not necessarily mean that the eagles of The Lord of the Rings are golden eagles.

Named after Something

From memes to video games to politics, Tolkien's legacy can be felt across all corners of popular culture, especially when it comes to naming things. In 2022, scientists named a star they discovered Earendel after the Tolkien character who carries a sacred radiant jewel across the sky in "The Voyage of Éarendel the Evening Star." There are also at least seven asteroids named after members of the Fellowship of the Ring, as well as one named after Mithril and another named after Gollum. There is a minor planet called Hobbits, and a specific region on Pluto's moon Charon named Morder Macula. At least thirty different celestial bodies, planetary features, and features on Saturn's moon Titan have been named after characters or features in Tolkien's works.

Biologists have also had their fun with Tolkien names. Gollum has a species of fish named after him, and Sauron a species of beetle, while Shelob has a spider named after her. As recently as November 2024, scientists who reported finding two new freshwater snail species named one after Éowyn (*Idiopyrgus eowynae*) and the other after Meriadoc (*Idiopyrgus meriadoci*).

Perhaps one of the most bizarre instances was during Tolkien's lifetime, when a woman named Meriel Thurston reached out to him asking if it would be okay for her to name her herd of cattle after Rivendell. Tolkien obliged wholeheartedly and even offered a bit of information. "I am honoured by your letter, and quite willing that you should use the name Rivendell as a herd prefix," Tolkien wrote. "The elvish word for 'bull' doesn't appear in any published work; it was MUNDO."

LITERARY CONNECTIONS

Names mean quite a lot in Middle-earth. And when Éowyn disguises herself as a man to fight in the battle to free Gondor in *Return of the King*, she calls herself Dernhelm. The name comes from Old English roots. "Dern" means "hidden" or "concealed," and "helm" can literally mean "helmet" or symbolically mean "warrior." So Éowyn's pseudonym Dernhelm means "the concealed warrior."

Further Reading

For further context or information about any of the quotes in this book, either from Tolkien's letters or from the extensive Lord of the Rings universe, please visit the *Tolkien Gateway* website (https://tolkiengateway.net).

- *Anything You Can Imagine: Peter Jackson and the Making of Middle-earth.* By Ian Nathan. HarperCollins—Fans of the behind-the-scenes extras for the Peter Jackson films will be absolutely delighted with this book.
- *The Atlas of Middle-earth.* By Karen Wynn Fonstad. Houghton Mifflin—For those who just need to know the finer details. The math behind it all is done here for you as Fonstad breaks down the geography of Middle-earth.
- *J.R.R. Tolkien: A Biography.* By Humphrey Carpenter. Houghton Mifflin (US)—This one has it all. From start to finish, it's one of the most detailed accounts of Tolkien's life.
- *The Letters of J.R.R. Tolkien.* Edited by Humphrey Carpenter and Christopher Tolkien. Houghton Mifflin (US)—From The Professor himself, this is a must-read for the most avid of Tolkien fans. Those looking for a glimpse into the life of one of the greatest authors of all time: This is for you.
- *The Lord of the Rings: A Reader's Companion.* By Wayne G. Hammond and Christina Scull. Houghton Mifflin

(US)—The ultimate way to read or re-read The Lord of the Rings is with this book. Find new insights into the trilogy, the structure of the story, and the meaning behind it all.

- *Middle-earth from Script to Screen: Building the World of The Lord of the Rings and The Hobbit.* By Daniel Falconer and Kellie Rice. HarperCollins—From the people who helped create the world of Middle-earth, this is a remarkably in-depth look at the world within Tolkien's mind.
- *The Road to Middle-earth: How J.R.R. Tolkien Created a New Mythology.* By Tom Shippy. Mariner Books (paperback edition)—Go back to the roots of it all as Tom Shippy masterfully examines the foundations of Middle-earth. Written by the man who got Tolkien's job after The Professor retired.
- *Tolkien and The Great War: The Threshold of Middle-earth.* By John Garth. HarperCollins—The horrors and heroism of war are found within these pages. Garth weaves a tale in this Tolkien biography of tragedy and imagination.
- *Tolkien's Faith: A Spiritual Biography.* By Holly Ordway. Word on Fire—For those wanting to explore The Professor's faith more deeply, look no further.
- *Why We Love Middle-earth: An Enthusiast's Book about Tolkien, Middle-earth, and the LotR Fandom (A Middle-earth Treasury).* By Shawn E. Marchese and Alan Sisto. Mango—Discover everything about Middle-earth—and then some! This book is a celebration of all things Tolkien, perfect for readers who want a delightful look at this wonderful fantasy world.

Index

U

V

W

Z

About the Author

DON MARSHALL, known as The Obscure Lord of the Rings Facts Guy across the Internet, has been inspiring fans and the nerd world at large with his Tolkien tidbits for years. With a decade of experience working in radio and television, Don's skills have segued into a very successful TikTok account, which reached viral status in 2020 and continues to entertain and inform the Tolkien fandom at large. Outside of his Tolkienian interests, Don enjoys writing, playing video games, and spending time with his wife, Nat Marshall; their dogs, River and Lucy; and their tortoise, Wash.

About the Illustrator

KIM ARRINGTON is an artist and illustrator living in Birmingham, Alabama. She primarily paints in watercolor and gouache, and sketches with ink, graphite, and colored pencils, creating loose and whimsically detailed images. Her simple joys in life are reading, drinking coffee, gardening, traveling, sketching, and spending time with her husband and four daughters.